night_sky

night_sky

FicSci 02

Edited by
Mehita Iqani and Wamuwi Mbao

AFRICAN
MINDS

Published in 2024 by African Minds
4 Eccleston Place, Somerset West, 7130, Cape Town, South Africa
info@africanminds.org.za | www.africanminds.org.za

ISBN (paper): 978-1-928502-92-0
eBook edition: 978-1-928502-93-7
ePub edition: 978-1-928502-94-4

Copies of this book are available for free download at: www.africanminds.org.za

ORDERS:
African Minds
Email: info@africanminds.org.za

To order printed books from outside Africa, please contact:
African Books Collective
PO Box 721, Oxford OX1 9EN, UK
Email: orders@africanbookscollective.com

Table of Contents

Acknowledgements vii

00 **Three Provocations and a Tweet** by Tana Joseph 001

01 **N//N; D//D** by Maneo Mohale 005

02 **Extragalactic Interruption** by Yolanda Mbelle 011

03 **Lost and Found** by Alicia English 027

04 **The Dark Heart of Everything** by Wamuwi Mbao 030

05 **Exchanges Unwritten and Unknown** by Eduardo Cachucho 036

06 **Three Poems** by Mathapelo Mofokeng 049

07 **Sky Counsel** by memory's daughter 053

08 **UMakhwezana** by Peggy Tunyiswa 063

09 **Four Poems** by Melissa Sussens 070

10 **Planisphærium Coeleste** by Skye Ayla Mallac 075

11 **Look Up! Don't Look Up!** by Mehita Iqani 081

12 **Forethought of Grief** by Sarah Uheida 095

13 **The Supernova Formula** by Mzwakhe Xulu 097

14 **Africatown** by Shamin Chibba 105

15 **As Above, So Below: Outroductory Reflections on FicSci 02**
by Wamuwi Mbao and Mehita Iqani 121

Biographies 126

Acknowledgements

FicSci is a not-for-profit academic research project that aims to produce and support experimental interdisciplinary encounters between science and creative writing. It is organised by the South African Research Chair in Science Communication and funded under the auspices of the National Research Foundation of South Africa.

FicSci is convened by Professor Mehita Iqani and Dr Wamuwi Mbao. For each workshop we choose a scientist specialist to invite to share their research. We are grateful to Dr Tana Joseph for sharing her knowledge and time for FicSci 02.

Each workshop invites select writers chosen through a competitive application process. We thank all the writers who accepted our invitation and shared three days of their lives with us to participate in this bold experiment.

We also thank Fumani Jwara and Elizabeth Newman for invaluable communications and logistical support on the project.

FicSci 02 was hosted at the Mont Fleur conference centre in the Blaauwklippen valley.

This anthology is available as an e-print for free download to reach the widest audience possible. It is published under a Creative Commons license.

*

Three Provocations and a Tweet

Tana Joseph

FicSci 02 featured three presentations from the invited scientist.

X-Ray Binary Stars

An x-ray binary star comprises a pair of gravitationally bound stars and one of the stars is a black hole or a neutron star (generally called compact objects). X-ray binaries emit all types of light, but their peak emission is in the x-rays, which is where they get their name. X-ray binaries are useful in the study of the universe because they are the only types of binary stars that we can see outside of the local group (which is the fifty galaxies including our own closest to Earth, our point of observation of the universe). X-ray binaries can be formed in two ways: the stars are born together as twins, then co-evolve until one ends up as a white dwarf or supernova, or they are formed from dynamical interactions, for example if they smash into each other and then become gravitationally linked. In stellar evolution, the smaller the mass of a star the longer it lives. Bigger stars burn through fuels more quickly such that their centres collapse more quickly too. While smaller stars burn more slowly and therefore last longer. In x-ray binary formations, a neutron star or black hole pulls off material from a companion (donor) star, which donates its material to grow a compact object. The lifetime of the donor star therefore sets the lifetime of the binary. Stars can lose mass either from the gravitational pull of the linked compact object, or from their inherent dense winds. About 2000 ultra-luminous x-ray binaries have been observed in the universe so far. They were first seen telescopically in the 1980s, and the sources were so bright that it was assumed the compact objects must be eight to ten times the mass of our sun. Better data updated that assumption to reveal that they were binary stars.

Reference: Joseph, Tana. "A Study of X-ray Binaries in the Local Universe." PhD thesis, University of Southampton, 2013. https:// eprints.soton.ac.uk/354111/

An Intriguing Source in M82

An intriguing source was noticed in M82, a nearby, prolific star-forming galaxy, regularly monitored by various observatories. Following up on a supernova explosion, astronomers wanted to see what was behind it, the shape of the explosion and how it interacted with the galaxy around it. This was when they discovered a faint radio source, which showed up in both x-ray and radio data, but the x-rays were strangely faint compared to what we expected when we extrapolated from how bright the radio emission was. The source was observed as becoming surprisingly bright quite quickly, and then staying constant for half a year. They measured it again a year later and it appeared to be getting brighter. When they looked at archival data from a week before the initial supernova explosion, there was no sign of this mysterious source. The chances of seeing a star system switch on are minimal, so this was an exciting moment. An infrared image of the galaxy where the source is located showed a cloud of gas around the object. The puzzle was to try and calculate what it could be. It was too faint to be a type of supernova, even taking into account the fact that the gas surrounding the object would block a lot of the light emitted from the source. The way it moves in time and its peak energy outputs don't line up with the best studied microquasar, so that was also ruled out. It is agreed that the source is some kind of x-ray binary star, but its exact nature is still uncertain.

Reference: Joseph, Tana D., Maccarone, T. J., and Fender, R. P. "The Usual Radio Transient in M82: An SS 43 Analogue?" *Monthly Notices of the Royal Astronomical Society: Letters* 415, no. 1 (July 2011): L59–63. https://arxiv.org/pdf/1107.4988.pdf

Magellanic Clouds

If you went outside in an area not overwhelmed by man-made night lighting somewhere in the southern hemisphere and looked up at the night sky, with the naked eye you might see formations that look like faint, blurry clouds. These are the Magellanic Cloud galaxies. They have been described as a binary because they are gravitationally bound and interacting, and one pulls matter from the other. There are two Magellanic Clouds that we can see from Earth, and they're named the Small (which is further away and less massive) and Large (which is closer and more massive) Magellanic Clouds respectively. Due to their gravitational interactions with each other and our galaxy, the Clouds are in the process of being pulled apart and deformed. This gives them their irregular shapes. One of the big questions in studying these Clouds is whether they are satellites of our galaxy. In other words, do they have a fixed orbit that moves around our galaxy, or are they just moving past on a trajectory of their own? There is evidence for both theories. The Clouds are also interesting because these galaxies are forming stars at a very rapid rate, especially high mass stars. Astronomers are interested in star formation because such observations can help us learn about the early universe. Working with MeerKAT data, the research tried to detect low-mass binary stars in the Magellanic Clouds. The data showed evidence of the remains of a supernova explosion and materials that should have disappeared after the explosion but didn't. This is the subject of ongoing study.

This work has not been published yet. But here's a link to some related work by researchers in South Africa using the Southern African Large Telescope (SALT) in the Karoo: Gvaramadze, V. V., A. Y. Kniazev, J. S. Gallagher, L. M. Oskinova, Y-H. Chu, R. A. Gruendl, and I. Y. Katkov. "SALT Observations of the Supernova Remnant MCSNR J0127–7332 and Its Associated Be X-Ray Binary SXP 1062 in the SMC." *Monthly Notices of the Royal Astronomical Society* 503, no. 3 (May 2021): 3856–66. https://academic.oup.com/mnras/article/503/3/3856/6164863

A Tweet

I look at dead stars in space. How do they form? From a big star that bursts at the end of its life. How do they shine? The dead star has a live star that is near, they are in a dance. The dead star pulls gas from the live star to make it shine. I look at the sky & I learn.

@TanaDJoseph (Twitter/X)

1

N//N; D//D

Maneo Mohale

I was really inspired by Dr Tana Joseph's visualisations and descriptions of x-ray binary star systems. It made me wonder how I could represent these gorgeous stellar systems on a formal and structural level within my poetry.

Here are two poems that mimic the dual structure and accretion of binary star systems. One poem, playfully titled "NEUTRAL WORDS//NEUTRON STAR" is a language-game (à la Wittgenstein), inspired by Dr Joseph's tweet-poem (see p. 4), wherein she uses monosyllabic words to describe the nature of her research. As an homage to (and a playful one-upping of) Dr Joseph's tweet-poem, "N//N" uses and collects bi-syllabic words spoken during Dr Joseph's provocations and arranges these words into octosyllabic strings.[1] I've found that the poem reveals its face best when spoken aloud.

The second piece is titled "DEATH-MOUTH//DONOR-STAR". As "N//N"'s companion, "D//D" is written as the piece's donor star, more massive in its structure. It is a prose poem / micro-fiction hybrid, featuring a bigender character named Nova.

---

1   No real reason why I settled on 8 syllables per line, I just think eight is a pretty number, and sounds delicious when spoken out loud. Octosyllabic lines feature all over my poetry. There's just something intuitively hypnotic about eights, no? Musical too.

NEUTRAL WORDS//NEUTRON STAR

"What words do you chant into the space between spaces, to bend your desires into reality?"
  — *Akwaeke Emezi, 'Dear Nonso'*

nothing. limit. noble. meerKAT.
someone. at night. nearby. useful.
suspect. study. data. donor.
transfer. differ. borrow. mimic.

index. early. spectral. standard.
alive. subtle. ion. under.
magnet. order. excess. X-S.
x-ray. X-1. access. process.

outside. cover. making. cluster.
swallow. orbit. forming. event.
ignore. super. impose. affect.
index. unit. double. direct.

flower. extend. pulsar. lighthouse.
smaller. longer. bigger. brighter.
system. cover. occam's. razor.
low mass. before. early. what form.

insight. data. optic. idea.
image. rule out. frequent. observe.
ASKAP. emit. a pulse. archive.
parts shaped. moving. big noise. research.

doctor. wobble. edit. cold beam.
metal. accrete. donor. nova.
outsee. object. compact. magnet.
inter. brightness. mega. translate.

ticking. relate. old clock. compact.
fourteen. great star. cosmos. focus.
smaller. hotter. thermal. direct.
expand. capture. exchange. action.

ion. collapse. assume. rapid.
destroy. vary. single. black hole.
instead. trench-coat. neutron. body.
presence. surface. mostly. unlike.

super. interest. explode. region.
eighty. receive. quasar. quasi.
stellar. measure. first thought. until.
we have. X-3. one such. micro.

brightness. figure. peak flux. some kind.
photons. Cygnus. detect. lol, where?
knowing. wisdom. richer. per cent.
they found. any. naming. question.

old thing. new school. partner. karoo.
countries. backyard. hub of. contact.
homage. working. sexy. light year.
bonus. infra. red-blue. compare.

colour. baby. motion. current.
test bed. southern. survey. have to.
timeline. can be. propose. sixty.
it took. remnant. effect. beauty.

result. quantum. changing. primer.
translate. emit. wispy. pulsar.
city. dyson. rotate. the sound.
famous. tease out. merger. the source.

become. dilate. deal with. something.
detail. fixture. large-small. heaven.

DEATH-MOUTH//DONOR-STAR

"Don't we deserve someone who puts us in their mouth slowly?"
—Akwaeke Emezi, *'Dear Senthuran'*

nova likes to think in cosmic time.

ever since she was a little boy, nova listened for the ticking. at first, time made a nothing sound. it clustered itself in the space between seconds, gathered in metallic filaments, as if by a magnet. as a boy, she'd often fall asleep against her grandfather's clock, listening for the ticking—tiny linear units of time, drumming themselves loose from the wood. she'd mimic Malome's clock, timing each tick with a doctor's devotion, ear positioned stethoscopically, imagining the clock alive. it was there, against the wood, that she learned the sacred rules of the universe:

> (1) everything with a heart is alive, (2) everything alive
> has a pulse and (3) everything with a pulse, keeps time.

in the winter of her 32nd year, nova traded her baby-brown ears for 64 massive mechanical eyes—nestled carefully in the karoo's low, dry grass. her eyes stretched themselves 13.5 metres wide: pale and metallic, each fitted with a cryogenic receiver. she liked the look of them. how they seemed to stare at the sky in chorus, their concave dishes and receivers raised aloft, gazing beyond the quiet into the mouths of dead and dying stars.

nova still listens for the ticking.

only now, time makes a scruffy sound: granular pulses made fuzzy by space-stuff and unfathomable distance. her desert eyes let her focus. through them, she observes and intuits the motion of a distant star in the crab nebula, a star the size of a city, nestled in ribbons of ancient gas and primordial ash. a pulsar in a crab-shaped cloud of gas, thousands of light years across, pincers glowing with mysterious mass and dust.

as her star turns, like a bulb in a lighthouse, it pulses in nova's direction in regular flashes of radiation, keeping sidereal time.

the pulsar's heartbeats make mercifully predictable patterns: rhythmic bright pulses and faint inter-pulses. in nova's data—each pulse rises as a sharp peak, hills rising high above her y-axes, always about 800 milliseconds apart. like many scientists before her and beyond her, she found the bursts of cosmic energetic emission to be reassuringly regular.

when granted telescope time, nova translates the data in rapid intuitive calculations, cleaning up the signal's peaks and troughs, stretching information out like a cloth, deciphering & anticipating the great star's movements.

i'd rather set my heart to a pulsar, than any clock on earth: what sahdi liked to say. and though they didn't share a lab together anymore— or a bed—nova tended to agree. her crab pulsar rotated on its axis thirty times every second, despite being incredibly dense and incredibly wide. even the fastest thing in the universe, a beam of light, would take ten years to cross from one end to another. *i'd rather set my heart—*

nova flexed her right hand, her body already stiff after hours of solitary scribbling. she always missed sahdi when she was tired. back when they were lab-mates, sahdi scanned and studied distant regions in space rich with binary star systems. soon after she arrived at meerKAT from mauritius, sahdi eventually settled her own desert eyes on Circinus X-1—an x-ray binary star system centred around a neutron star.

sahdi liked watching the slow dance the two stars performed in the sky. she'd speculate on how their orbit would decay over time, flirting with quantum equations when thinking about the stretchy squishiness of spacetime around mega massive objects in the sky. nova & sahdi would spend hours in animated conversation, adjusting and comparing models, reviewing research, often collapsing into soft, comfortable silences. nova loved the moments when their models would match up, when the data and their predictions would match *just* so. it was the part of the work that made astronomy feel like time-twisted prophecy.

they found that they fell in love slowly—having rotated each other for a year in shy, slow arcs. nova remembered the feeling of sahdi's wood-brown body against her own, the precise angle of her head on her own jittery chest. how her breath would pool below her adam's apple.

sahdi would lay her lips at the centre of nova's chest until her heart calmed, entropy finally put to good use. they'd swallow each other's brightness at night, locked tight in their own heavenly double-dance—the hub of nova's brain heated overwhelmingly with sensation and fleshy information.

in the morning, when the source of nova's anxiety would descend upon her like a wispy-weighted trench-coat, adding gravel to her voice, sahdi would console her with stories about the sun. *she's five-billion years old already, our girl. and already halfway through her life-cycle. in her death-days, she'll cool into a red giant, swelling so far beyond her current size that the earth will be eaten. in another five-billion years, any trace of us will be gone. any trace of any of us. it's all ephemeral, sweetboy.*

surrounded by ephemera, and the fleeting touch-timed nature of everything, nova let her mind cool itself against the memory of sahdi's deep, southern-tipped voice. she thought in cosmic time. in billions and trillions and many, many orders of ten, impossible units of space-time, until the large-small dread dulled itself to a murmur.

nova gathered her notes, and finally thought about going home. she flexed her right hand, once more. she walked quickly, drumming her fingers in regular rhythm, against her own sweet self.

2

Extragalactic Interruption

Yolanda Mbelle

1.

FADE IN:

1   EXT - KAROO DESERT WALK - DUSK   1

Xhaspha, a chubby, tall Seer walks as if drawn
by an invisible, yet powerful, string to hear
the gods in the silence of the desert. His
attention is pulled to the right of the field by
the enchanting smell of the lonesome Boswelia
tree. Xhaspha reaches for his pocket knife and
begins to cut off parts of the tree bark to make a
frankincense ointment. A handful later, he takes
in the fragrance of the frankincense with a deep
belly breath.

As he exhales, a force hits his chest, and he
gasps for air. In a panic, he struggles to stay
on his feet. He staggers as he tries to raise his
head to look up at the sky to pray for help from
his gods in the third heaven.

That is when he witnesses the starry explosion.
Xhaspha is the Seer of all Seers in the Khoi
region. He has full and unhindered access into

the third heaven where the gods reside. It is
here he often learns the agendas of heaven for
Earth. It is there where he collects messages
and delivers them to the people, speaking as
an oracle of the gods. In absolute shock and
anguish, he runs home.

FADE TO BLACK.

2.

2   EXT - DEEP SPACE   2

Beyond the Karoo moon, there is an alluring
soundlessness that seems to beckon one to embark
on a journey into the Milky Way. This way leads
to the Magellanic Clouds, a far distance away
from our Earth. The end of this first heaven is
enveloped by the vast silent darkness of space.

Diving deeper into the foreign blackness, a
freckle of light the size of a mustard seed
appears within this second heaven. As the eye
journeys on further into this newness, the speck
of light grows. The extragalactic growth of this
light births a prettily pigmented swirl around
the mouth of a very large light-consuming ditch.
This accretion disc twirls dreamingly into the
big Black Hole where no light can live.

A near distance away, a laddish star begins to
flirt with the sassy sparkly counterpart. She
yields. Stellar hand in stellar hand the happy
couple floats, lost in love, at close proximity to
the accretion disc, admiring its polychromatic
colours and soft textures. A beautiful binary
bond forms.

In an instant, the global cluster's serene
atmosphere is disrupted. In a split second, a

quasi-stellar invader staggering in drunkenness displaces the couple; the microquaser whizzes right between their binary bond, firing off energy and light so sharp it shoots off like a jet engine.

At this, the happy stellar couple is violently pulled away from each other and spins off in different directions. The laddish bigger star is losing his energy rapidly and is giving up the hope of reuniting with the love it once knew. The sassy smaller star knows nothing else but to fight. She is shooting straight back into the stellar arms she has grown to love so much, but to no avail.

This extragalactic interruption sends very large flares of multi-coloured star lights into space, within the third heaven. This unchartered realm is reserved for the gods and celestial beings. Its majesty cannot be denied.

FADE OUT.

3.

3   EXT. KAROO NATIONAL PARK -
      CONFERENCE CENTRE - DAY 3

The super sterile atmosphere of the Karoo National Park is even heavier today due to the presence of the government special forces guarding the deputy president of South Africa and the other dignitaries accompanying him. Click click click click click click click resounds the battery of cameras of the gathered press. Everyone has come to experience the launch of the Karoo Array Telescope, fondly known as the KAT. The year is 2016. Minister Londeka Phakathi is on the podium, ready to address the people.

                    MINISTER LONDEKA PHAKATHI
          Mr Deputy President, distinguished
          guests, members of the press, ladies
          and gentlemen, people of the Northen
          Cape, this is a very proud moment for
          us all. I greet you all and welcome
          you to the launch of the Karoo Array
          Telescope.

(Applause and cheers)

          I apologize for the delay in our
          proceedings. As you know, the purpose
          of today's gathering was to launch
          the twenty receptors that make up
          KAT.

Crowd murmurs indignantly. They have heard enough
promises from the government about this project.
So far, nothing has come of it. They've been
told that this project is their only hope for
generating income for their families.

                    MINISTER LONDEKA PHAKATHI
          However, I stand before you now
          to announce that, together with
          parliament, President Matthew Rammusi
          - who couldn't be here with us today
          due to other obligations(louder
          murmurs, she talks over them in a
          much louder and excited tone)- has
          increased the budget for the building
          of 64 receptors instead. Yes, that's
          right, more KAT everyone, more KAT!
          (louder cheers and applause)

                    SOMEONE IN THE CROWD(EXCITED)
          More KAT. More? *Sy bedoel meer, meer*
          --- Meer KAT.

(the crowd jubilates as they chant MeerKAT)

FADE TO:

3A   EXT. KAROO NATIONAL PARK - PAVILLION
3A

> NEWS REPORTER
> I'm reporting to you live from the
> Great Karoo Conference Centre at
> the Karoo National Park, where the
> minister of science and technology,
> Dr Londeka Phakathi, has just
> made a stellar announcement of an
> extragalactic nature. Today marks
> the launch of the Karoo Array
> Telescope project, which was meant to
> start building 20 receptors. These
> Northern Cape residents have eagerly
> anticipated this prospect as it is
> set to create hundreds of jobs in the
> community. Minister Phakathi was a
> little late in coming onto the podium
> and met with an agitated audience.
> And of course, the community was
> indignant because many promises have
> been made regarding this project over
> the years, only to be disappointed
> with more postponements. This time
> though, the agitation turned to
> complete jubilation, when she more
> than tripled the budget allocated
> for the project. KAT technology or
> MeerKAT, as the locals now call it,
> is the first of its kind worldwide
> and will help our scientists and
> astronomers delve deeper into their
> study of space and possibly explore
> further than anyone has ever been
> able to. This is ---

As Londeka Phakathi, Daniel Sibiya (deputy
president of South Africa) and their entourage
wave to the people as they move to the dining

hall, the crowd's singing and cheers drown out
the reporter's voice.

                    CROWD(LOUDLY CHEERS)
          MeerKAT, MeerKAT, MeerKAT, MeerKAT,
          MeerKAT, MeerKAT, MeerKAT, MeerKAT

The government officials go on to shake hands
with the astronomers that will be working with
MeerKAT. Jabu, the junior intern pushes his way
to the front to get a handshake too. This team
will be the very first in the world to use this
kind of technology. Everyone is excited to see
what possibilities lie within our own and beyond
other galaxies.

FADE TO BLACK.

4.

4   INT. Seer's Consultation Room   4

Xhaspha staggers into his consultation room,
grabs his prayer shawl from the table and covers
his head as he kneels. A few seconds later, he
raises his head and places the shawl on his
shoulders. There is an empty calabash next to
him, and a bucket of water right next to it. He
hurriedly draws out the water into the calabash.
He covers his head and the calabash with the
shawl as he chants and prays to the gods to
confirm his vision.

                    XHASPHA
          Xhkha ra xhGaboo tsi xhgu xhKhoo tsa
          xhGaeb   (Thank the gods who guide and
          protect us).

The vision appears in the water-filled calabash.
It is an extragalactic interruption, an exchange
interaction that cannot be avoided and definitely

cannot be ignored. In the language of the gods, Xhaspha gives thanks.

                    XHASPHA
          Xhkha ra xhGaboo (Thank the gods).

He removes his prayer shawl and steps out of the room, grabs his phone and dials Xhola's number. The call goes straight to voicemail.

Xhola lost both parents to AIDS when she was only 4 years old. Xhaspha's parents took her in, as she was already very fond of her cousin. They became a close-knit family; and Xhola referred to Xhaspha's parents as mum and dad instead of aunt and uncle. The two were the same age and grew up more as twins than cousins. They are inseparable.

Xhaspha puts the phone in his pocket and hurries outside after removing his shoes. He steps onto the ground and covers his head with the prayer shawl. He repeats the prayer and chants. He bends over and gathers a chunk of soil in his hands. He repeats the chants then examines the soil in his palms. He is shaken by what he sees and gently returns the soil where he found it, thanking the gods.

                    XHASPHA
          Xhkha ra xhGaboo (Thank the gods).

Xhaspha decides to send a text message to his beloved cousin, Xhola. He starts typing:

    *Xhgaboo (greetings), Xho. Urgently call me
    please cuz. Especially before you go to your
    person. CALL ME.
    (frustrated emoji)
    Why is your phone off? Call me. Urgently.
    It's Xhaspha.*

(pauses then continues muttering to himself)

*The elements have spoken. The stars, the
earth and the water are in agreement. Xho,
we must talk.*

FADE TO:

5.

5   INT. Selby's House - KITCHEN - NIGHT

Xhola and Selby are doing the dishes. They are
playful and happy. Selby's phone buzzes. He grabs
it, reads the message and puts it back down and
continues to fool around with Xhola, causing
her to giggle joyously. They turn off the lights
and walk into the bedroom hand in hand. Xhola
releases her hand from his and walks into the
bathroom.

Selby quickly gets his phone and starts typing
frantically. He is done by the time Xhola
reappears. Xhola, now dressed only in Selby's
T-shirt, jumps into bed and motions Selby to
join. Selby hesitates.

                SELBY(NONCHALANT)
        That message was from Tayana. She
        says she urgently needs to speak to
        me. Let me quickly make the call.
        I'll be right back.

Tayana is Selby's ex-girlfriend. This disturbs
Xhola. She is left alone in the bedroom
questioning what just happened. She is paralyzed
for a moment.

                XHOLA(THOUGHTFUL)
        Why is he leaving the room to speak
        to his ex? This late at night?

Selby returns after the call and just slips into
bed without a word. Xhola is upset and lifts her
head from the pillow, giving Selby a disapproving
look.

>   SELBY(DISMISSIVE)
>   You must say if you don't want me to
>   talk to anyone on the phone.

>   XHOLA
>   Are you out of your mind? What a
>   nerve? How can ---

Selby pulling her out of bed with such great
force interrupts her indignation. She stumbles,
almost falling to the ground. Before she can
regain her balance, Selby throws her clothes
at her, yelling at her. He escorts her to the
kitchen door.

>   SELBY(ANGRY)
>   Don't talk to me like that in my own
>   house! Leave. Now.

>   XHOLA(PUZZLED)
>   What's happening? What are you doing?

Xhola tries to de-escalate the situation so they
can talk. She reaches for his hand to hold him.
Selby's hand gets scratched as he violently pulls
away from her.

>   SELBY(FUMING)
>   You're asking for a fight. I said go.
>   You are now trespassing. Leave my
>   house now.

Selby looks at his hand and notices the scratch.
He pushes Xhola out the kitchen door.

                    SELBY(FURIOUS)
          You just assaulted me. Look what you
          did to my hand. That's it. You will
          have the police to answer to. I've
          had it.

He slams the kitchen door shut leaving Xhola
outside, still half dressed.

FADE OUT.

5A   EXT. SELBY'S HOUSE - FRONT YARD - NIGHT
5A

Xhola is standing outside Selby's kitchen door
shocked at what has just happened. Just then a
bright spotlight shines on her half-naked body.

                    SECURITY GUARD(CONFUSED)
          Who are you? We received a call about
          a trespasser at this address. What
          are you doing here?

Xhola shields her eyes from the piercing light
with one hand. The rest of the clothes she had
in that hand fall to the ground. Her hapless
tears follow the same trail. Without a word
she slowly puts her pants on. She picks up her
phone from the ground and requests an Uber ride.
The security guard is sympathetic and tries to
console her so he can get a full understanding
of the situation. Xhola is crying silently and
does not respond to anything he says. The Uber
arrives. Moving slowly, she makes her way to the
silver Toyota Agya that's come to collect her.

She picks up the remainder of her clothes
(jacket, socks, shoes, bra) from the ground. She
walks past the security guard towards the Uber.
Her bra falls out of her hand. She picks it up
along with the shreds of dignity she has left.

As she reaches for the backseat door, her jacket
falls to the ground; she surrenders to her tears.

The security guard picks it up and opens the Uber
door for her. Head hanging in shame, she enters
the car and nods her head for the driver to
leave. She sobs as the car drives off.

FADE TO BLACK.

6.

6   INT. MEERKAT CONTROL ROOM - EARLY EVENING 6

Meerkat National Park, home of the world-class
MeerKAT radio telescope launched by Dr Londeka
Phakathi a few months ago, is tucked away snuggly
in South Africa's Northern Cape. The parched
Karoo landscape boasts vast open plains with the
clearest night skies hovering above. Our Milky
Way, with all its splendour, overlays the night
sky. The naked eye easily spots the Magellanic
Clouds; while the iris of the radioscope, the
MeerKAT, the only one of its kind, sees beyond
the first heaven that no other radioscope has ever
been able to reach. This time though, an unusual
wave of radio activity appears on the monitors
at the MeerKAT station control room accompanied
by beeping sounds of the machine's alarms. The
captain and his team all huddle around their
screens for a closer look. There it is: an
interaction exchange never before recorded. An
extragalactic interruption. Jabu, the overzealous
junior intern is the first to speak excitedly.

                JABU(CURIOUS)
        Captain Kruger, Sir? Do you see? Are
        you looking at the screen?

The captain's eyes are already on the screen. He
walks to the bigger monitor and disregards Jabu.

                    CAPTAIN KRUGER(CAUTIOUSLY EXCITED)
          Blow up that image. Hurry. Zoom in.
          More. More dammit come on. Meer.

The room is pregnant with exhilaration. The air
in the room grows thick with anticipation. The
astronomers gather around the big screen barely
containing their excitement as they observe the
grand fireworks display. This is the very first
deep space odyssey of its kind captured by any
telescope. They all break out into joyous cheers.
They just witnessed and recorded an extragalactic
binary star interruption millions of light years
away in what Xhaspha and the Khoi Seers call the
third heaven.

FADE TO BLACK.

7.

7   INT. XHOLA'S HOUSE - BEDROOM - NIGHT   7

Xhola is in a daze, lost in thought, confused.
She glances at her phone and notices a message
from her cousin. Without listening she dials his
number.

               XHASPHA
          Xhkha ra xhGaboo (Thank the gods).
          Finally you return my call. Listen to
          me very carefully.

          (pause)

          (Xhola sniffles between silent sobs.)

          Xhola? Xhola, are you crying? Oh no.
          So you didn't get my message? Is it
          Selby? Please tell me he didn't hurt
          you. Xhola, xhaab kabba xhkaam(Hush,

my baby). Do you want me to come
over?

          XHOLA
Too many questions, Xhas! I have my
own too. Tayana, the ex. Why is she
calling all of a sudden? Then tell me
who that man I was with just now is.
I think I went to the wrong house.
Where is my Selby? What happened?

          XHASPHA
The stars, the water and the ground
gave the warning. Unfortunately, I
could not reach you in time to give
it. Come to think of it, I don't
think there was anything anyone could
have done to stop this. I thank the
gods that I could see it. But they
didn't show me that it could be
avoided. It was written in the stars.
I'm here to help you put the pieces
back together again, cuz. That is
all I can do. Until the stardust has
settled, there's nothing anyone can
do for you.

          XHOLA(UPSET)
Xhas, I'm not one of your clients.
Give it to me straight. We both knew
it was too good to be true anyway. So
spare me the gods' mumbo jumbo.

          XHASPHA(SYMPATHETIC)
But why did he lie the first time
around? He said he was in this for
the long haul. Then he starts to
change when you mention your illness?
And I tried to tell you to watch him.
You kept ---

XHOLA

Yes, yes, yes. I know. I kept saying
he meant it. He would be with me even
through the illness. But obviously he
was just looking for a way out. So
Tayana made for the perfect excuse.
And I remember that look on your face

XHASPHA(PUZZLED)

Uhm --- that I could see it?

XHOLA

That it was too good to be true. He
doesn't seem like the type to feed
you soup when you're bedridden by
illness. You've always said the man
was emotionless --- (sobs)

XHASPHA(CONSOLING)

Xho, you always see the good in
people. You felt enough love for the
both of you. You had no idea he'd
left you the day he realised ---

XHOLA

--- I was damaged? I have a disease.
Is that a crime? Many couples live
with HIV for many decades with no
complications. I was born with it and
have not had any trouble since.

XHASPHA

Yes. But not everyone is educated
enough on this subject. You did well
by letting him know. I know you
are in pain. And your world seems
shattered. But the stardust will
settle. And I'm here all the way.

FADE TO BLACK.

8.

8   INT. MEERKAT CONTROL ROOM   8

Captain Kruger is hunched before his computer
screen, replaying the scenes from the
extragalactic eruption with a smile. He studies
the waves and other readings. Suddenly something
on the readings seems to catch his attention.

              CAPTAIN KRUGER(ADDRESSING ALL)
              If this extragalactic display is as
              I have calculated, then the stardust
              should be settling today. We have
              to launch the MeerKAT towards the
              coordinates of the event right
              away. We could witness a stardust
              spectacle.

Jabu, the curious intern, walks towards the
captain and looks him right in the eye.

              CAPTAIN KRUGER
              Was I not clear? Why do you all just
              stand there? Launch. That's an order!

After a few clicks on the keyboard, there is an
unfamiliar celestial sound and wave pattern. A
few more clicks give a better view of deep space.
The celestial music is dreamy and whimsical.
There seems to be very fine starry rain in the
third heaven. It is fine stardust.

Asteroseismology is born. The stardust waltzes to
the music creating a curiously beautiful newness
that is yet to be named. The dust twirls, sways,
leaps and curtsies in a celestial choreography.
The dust whirls and whirls; then particles
periodically touch each other painting the
tapestry of space with colours not yet seen by
any mortal eye. The astronomers are all in awe as
they watch this symphony of lights.

                    CAPTAIN KRUGER(IN A WHISPER)
          I shall name this Stardust Spectacle.

FADE OUT.

9.

9   EXT. XHOLA'S HOUSE - OUTSIDE GATE   9

Xhola opens the gate to enter the yard when the
sound of a car startles her. She looks back to
see Selby in the driver's seat. They both stare
at each other for a moment. No one speaking.

They both seem to stop breathing when their eyes
connect. Simultaneously, Xhola opens the gate
again and runs towards Selby; and Selby opens
his car door and runs towards Xhola. The two of
them embrace. Selby gently caresses Xhola's belly
before bending down to kiss it.

Some of the stardust particles produced through
the galactic explosion begin to settle on one
another, attempting to reignite the bond that
once was. She smiles. There is stardust in her
eyes. Oh it burns, yet she smiles still.

                    SELBY(EMOTIONAL)
          Hello, SJ.

                    XHOLA(CONFUSED)
          SJ?

                    SELBY
          Yes. Selby Junior. Daddy's here.

The couple embraces once again and waltzes to
an imaginary song.

FADE TO BLACK.

END OF EPISODE

3

Lost and Found

Alicia English

It seems like a million light years away now, but I can still remember the day our worlds collided. After our first encounters, I intrinsically knew that our lives would inevitably be joined together. I thought our symphony would go on forever. You had so much love, light and life to give. You always gave of yourself, yet very few people knew that you were the star that gave of itself so that I could continue shining. You gave and gave, until there was nothing more of yourself to give, or of your life left to live.

Surrounded always by a myriad of stars, I have never felt more alone. Confusing right? Our children remind me of you, but they are not you. I am on my own. Alone with my thoughts, my questions, my dreams. Alone with my fears, my folly, my secret sins. I am alone with my dark passions, my desires, this unending aching in my bones to be with you.

Oh flesh of my flesh, bone of my bones …

I am a lone, dwindling star, drifting daily between time and space. I hide behind the grandeur of excellence in my craft, my courage in times of adversity and my boisterous laughter. Every now and then single parenthood gifts me bursts of joy and splendour. Unbeknownst to many, they stem from the catastrophic eruption of my world as I knew it, much like a supernova. Some are fooled by the surge of bright light, not knowing how deep my pain really runs.

Exhale.

Sometimes I think it would have been better if I were on a collision course with a new star.

If my heart was captured by another to form a new identity, perhaps then I could find peace again. But that is not the portion set aside for me by fate. Mine is to drift away.

Sometimes I wish a passing star's gravitational pull would draw me into its embrace and comfort my aching soul. But that is not my portion either. Instead everything tied to this life I once knew is being ripped apart by the tidal force of an emotional black hole.

Last night I looked out through the window, hoping to see the radiance of your light in the expanse of the cold dark sky. I could find no trace of you there. I listened for the sound of your voice calling my name. Nothing. Complete radio silence.

I am caught in a spiralling ebb and flow of emotions. I've been displaced from you—my centre. You've become a transient object of my affection that now only lives in my memory. And that scares me. What happens when my memory fades and I can't recall how once we were bound together?

We are worlds apart. I wish you were here, but there's nothing I can do about it.

Exhale.

Yesterday I wept. Not for losing you, but for losing myself in the aftermath of your death.

Not because of what is no more, but for the reality that can now never be.

I cried because the life we built together now lay in ruins. All I could see was dust and gas—the only remnants of our perfectly imperfect galaxy exploding.

But today is a new day. It is a new dawn, and I am thankful.

I am thankful for the confusion because from it I can reach a new sense of clarity, and for the pain because through it I can discover a strength I never knew I had.

I am thankful for the inner wounds because they teach me that sometimes healing does not only require time—sometimes you need to travel the distance in light years to find it.

I am thankful for the radio silence because in it I am learning to tune into the frequency of my soul and listen out with hopeful expectation. I am confident that the waves of wisdom—though imperceptible to my naked eye and ears—travel through time and space and will inevitably reach me at God's appointed time.

I am thankful because now that I have wrestled with and confronted my emptiness, I can look it dead in the eyes and command, "Emptiness be filled!"

I am thankful: my new star could not be born without the dust and gas that are all that remains of you.

I am ever-changing, ever renewing, ever reborn.

4

The Dark Heart of Everything

Wamuwi Mbao

Incident on a dark night. 3am, December the 24th. Most people safely in bed or else seeing out a sleepy nightshift before heading home to their families. Hesperus Coetzee was dieseling slowly along the top of a rocky ridge that stuck up from the landscape. The squeaky bakkie made furrows in the dirt. Meera Swartz in the seat next to him was frowning out into the darkness. The two patrollers had been combing the area, and on the wide-shot horizon there was the thinnest streak of what would be light in an hour or two. The stars were buckshot into the inky blue night as though the dark was just a blanket beyond which an all-encompassing brilliant light lay waiting.

"What do you think it was?" Meera started to enter the checkpoint into the ledger, but the lead point of the pencil snapped. She glared at it, then tossed it out into the gloom and whistled the first bars of *Let's Face the Music and Dance*.

"You shouldn't litter," Hesperus said.

Meera sighed, "Nothing out here but quiver trees and porcupines." She was not quite right. A great deal happened, but very little of it was visible if you weren't looking through a telescope, staring at screens, comparing charts, or doing equations. The hum of activity that surrounded the SKA contrasted somewhat with the town itself, which was sinking slowly into the shabby Karoo poverty that was the style of the time. The arrival of 64 imposing satellite telescopes had briefly boosted town morale. People had applauded in the main street as the massive white satellite dishes were trucked past. And they had applauded under a malevolent sun while the deputy president and the ministers and the scientists weaved them a narrative about the reality going on above their heads, and about how the machines would be for seeing, but also a kind of listening as well.

If the Deputy President was to be believed, then the arrival of the satellites would turn the town into a tourist mecca. The promises had hung around about as long as the dust raised by the VIP motorcades as they retreated for softer parts of the world. The tainture of that fading hope was something Hesperus saw every day as he drove around the town. There had been a brief flurry of corbelled houses being converted to guest cottages on one side of the road, and the museum had been given a fresh coat of paint, but other than a steady stream of researchers and students, most of whom were pale and hermetic, little changed in the little town. Hesperus had traded patrolling farms and lodges for the rather more interesting day to day affair of keeping the stargazers safe. This involved patrolling the road to the base station, circling the maintenance route that ran out from the station to the dishes, occasionally delivering things to the bunker. Nothing too taxing.

Meera hated security duty at MeerKAT. The concrete computer room which received whatever the telescopes were seeing seemed to belong to in a Cold War movie about push-button warfare. For Hesperus, however, it was like driving through the gates of Troy. The site was 90 km out of Carnarvon, inconveniently far away, and especially so if an alarm should happen to go off at 1am on Christmas Eve. Hesperus had met the current cohort, and he knew that Pelser and Fortuin, the two SCOs from ETOS, were supposed to have left the centre on the morning of the 24th. As Hesperus had been able to ascertain, Pelser had called the patrol office to report that Fortuin had returned to the facility earlier that day, stating that he had to retrieve a hard drive he had left there, and hadn't returned. The office had in turn called Hesperus to request that a patrol vehicle be sent out to search the park and that patrol vehicle happened to be the one that Hesperus was steering over the scrubby plain.

"So you're telling me that these people spend all their time," Meera was saying, "looking for UFOs out here in the middle of nowhere?"

"I am telling you that, yes," Hesperus said. He was relaying to Meera, as he had been doing for the last hour, the conversations between himself and the now-missing fellow from the Extra-Terrestrial Observation Society. "Apparently, their money is essential to keeping this place going."

It wasn't unusual for the SCOs to remain past their stipulated leaving dates. Sometimes there were things that needed to be looked at more closely, with greater time and detail than the typical time frame would allow. One of the SCOs had explained to him, because he had asked, that the telescopes were never turned off.

"You can't turn off the sky, can you?" Fortuin had said. He had explained to Hesperus that ETOS kept its own bank of super computers in the bunker. Hesperus remembered that the conversation had been at once strange and ordinary, given the content.

"And an SCO ... ?" Meera asked.

"Secondary Commensal Observer," Hesperus pronounced each word significantly. "They piggyback off what the scientists do. So, if the telescopes are pointing in a particular direction, they spend their time looking there for the things they're interested in."

"Which would be?"

"Pulses. Or did he say pulsars? Radar signals. Things that go flash in the night." To Hesperus, who had grown up in the region, it seemed that the area was perfect for spotting unusual things amid the stars. For as long as he had been looking up, he had always been convinced that there were more stars than sky in their part of the world. As a child, the adults complained that the stars were so bright as to rob sleepers of their dreams. Even now, the mute glowing pinpricks so carpeted the vast night pitch that scarcely any dark could be seen. So who was he to say that there weren't other civilizations up there, trying to reach out?

The town was of little historical consequence until some accident of geography conspired to make the place ideal for starwatching of a monumental kind. The scientists had explained how their telescopes were part of an international network of other starwatchers, and Hesperus had felt a swelling of pride that his little town was known in some way internationally. It was hard to explain to anyone who had never lived there, Hesperus thought. Perhaps it would be hard to explain if you'd only lived there, too. The quiet and the dust and the heat get into your mind and all the cogs start to grind and destroy themselves. There was too much room for thinking, and too much space to disappear into. Perhaps you might decide to go out and see for yourself what was out there.

"When I was growing up," Meera said, "I watched a show on TV called *The Galaxy Rangers*. Whenever I hear these guys talk about neutrinos and parsecs, it's all I think about."

"You should bring that up with them," Hesperus said. "Although it might be somewhat before their time."

Nobody was currently at the ETOS computers that translated the frozen stars into science. When Hesperus and Meera arrived at the building, the front door was thrown open, yellow light streaming out onto the talc-like dust that carpeted the grounds. Someone had been and gone, briefly, hurriedly. A cupboard ajar, provisions rifled through and selected, screens and papers left as if someone had run out to attend to some unknown, unexpected visitor.

They had driven out, combing the dirt road between the station and the main cluster of telescopes, culling scrubby brushland under the wheels. They were trying to assemble some kind of picture for themselves of what had gone on in the night. No scientist. Nobody. Just the satellites looming on the landscape like a stilled amusement park. He stopped the bakkie some distance away from one of the dishes and they lowered the windows and they sat there with the coming morning condensing around them. With straining ears and eyes, they listened to the furtive clicks and twungs of cooling metal. A bird called a harsh and strange alarm at their presence. There were no human sounds in the air.

"Strange," said Meera. "I always expect them to make more noise than that."

"They're cooled by helium," Hesperus said. It was another of the things the missing ETOS fellow had told him.

They got out of the bakkie and stood leaning against the bonnet. They were attracting moths. He extinguished the lights and she said, "Do you think he hanged himself?"

Hesperus sighed.

"A night clear enough to count cows by," said Hesperus, "and a lost sky gazer somewhere in it." Something told him that the missing man was out here somewhere. That Fortuin had not wandered out randomly. That there was some purpose behind his disappearance.

He got out and peered out across the plain. As if cued by his leaving the car, an unseasonably cold wind blew across, scattering small tumbleweeds and whistling through the ladders and metalwork. A clatter of springboks took off across the plain, pursued by a blanket of cloud that dimmed the sky.

"My granny would call that a bad omen," Meera said quietly.

Hesperus was silent for a moment, listening to the wind and the notes it carried. "Just a phenomenon of nature with no one to report to." Suddenly, there was a tremendous clang, and from the darkness 50 m ahead of them, a figure began to descend from one of the towers.

Hesperus started in surprise, but Meera—always calmer—ducked below the silhouette of the bakkie. Hesperus followed suit. The figure stood looking in their direction, apparently not seeing them. Hesperus saw that they were eclipsed by the shadow of one of the dishes. The figure was now advancing towards them, his flashlight poor, his steps halting. Meera crept around the base of the tower as the man approached. In a couple of steps, he would notice the bakkie.

Hesperus tensed.

Meera sprang, knocking their quarry off his feet. There was a scuffle in the dark, and a cry of alarm from a voice Hesperus recognized.

"That's him!" He unclipped the torch from his belt and shone it at the scene that had unfolded near his feet. Meera had one of Fortuin's arms twisted behind his back. She pulled him to his feet and dusted him off. The SCO glared at them indignantly.

"Do you know that everybody's looking for you?" Meera scolded him. "They thought you were dead in a donga somewhere."

Fortuin looked wildly around him. "I was hiding, for your information." Hesperus saw that the man was shaken by something other than Meera's attack.

"Hiding from what?"

He looked at them suspiciously. "Someone was here in the bunker this morning. Two people in fact."

Hesperus said, "There shouldn't have been anyone here but the guards, and you."

"I know," Fortuin snapped. He was regaining his composure now that he felt safe. "I interrupted them. There had been a fight, I think. The one man hit the other over the head with a Maglite. Then he charged at me," he said, rubbing his shoulder. "I took off and locked the door behind me, but when I ran out, there were no guards, so I fled to the telescope because I figured a patrol car would come by eventually."

Hesperus and Meera stared at each other.

"Who was it?" Fortuin asked.

Hesperus took a breath. "There was nobody in the bunker. The door was open. And the guards didn't see anyone come or go."

"Why would I lie?" Fortuin pleaded.

Hesperus opened the door to the bakkie. "Hop in. Let's go and find out."

5

Exchanges Unwritten and Unknown

Eduardo Cachucho

Eon is a binary star - fits all the criteria for being one. Their ass is a blown out neutron star, has lobes for light years, and an accretion surface as curved as spacetime herself.

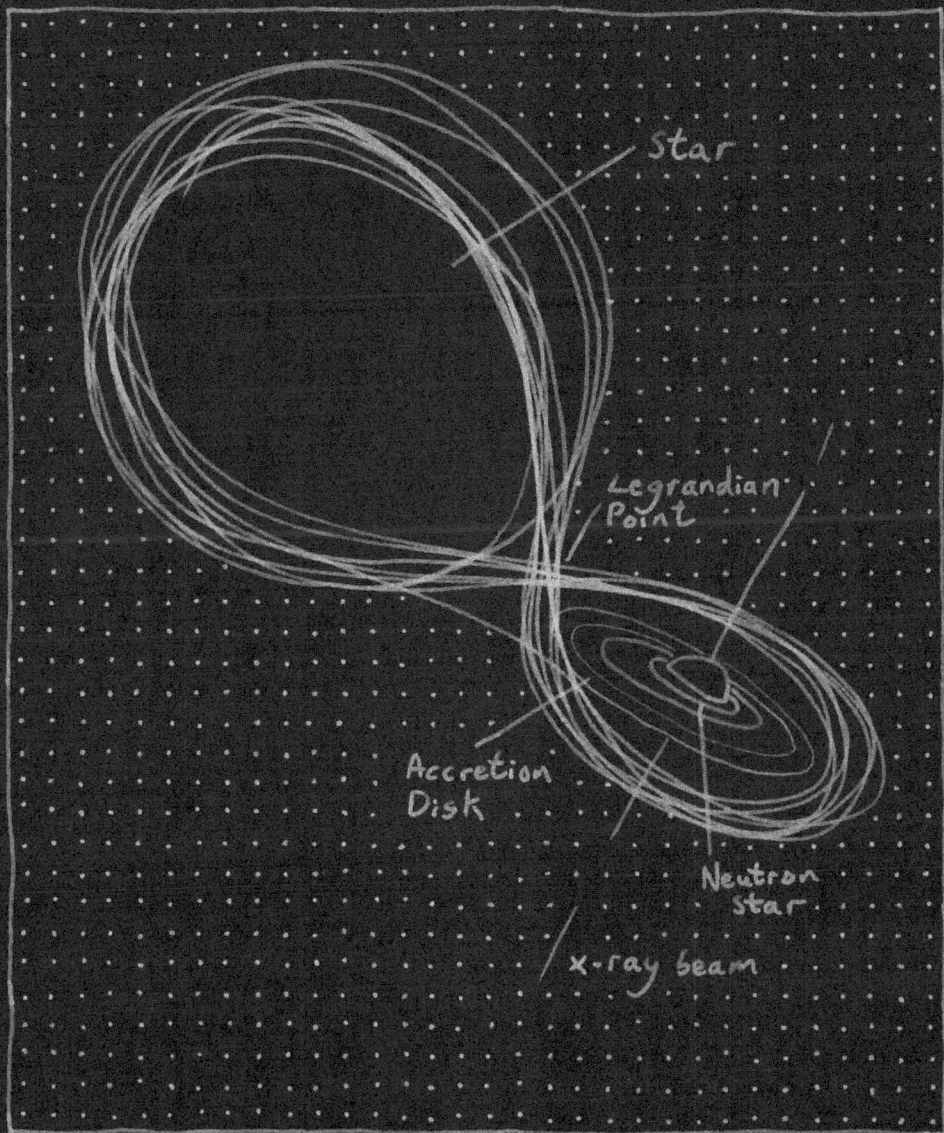

Star

Legrandian Point

Accretion Disk

Neutron Star

x-ray beam

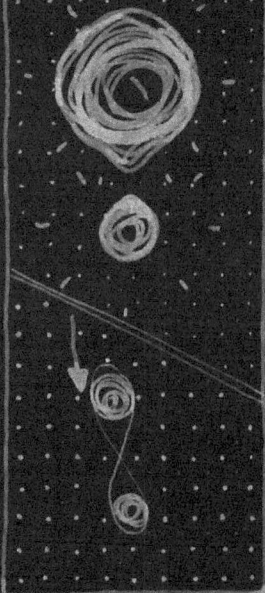

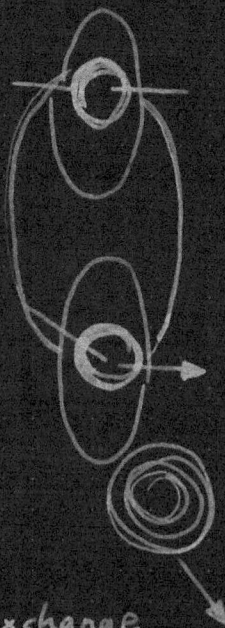

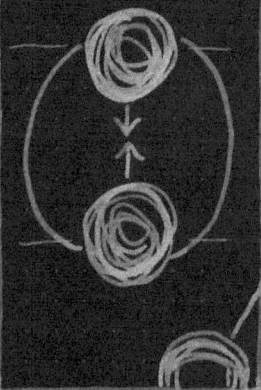

Pulsar

The universe's #1
stellar dating app

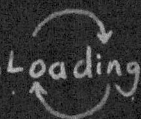

↻ Loading ↺

E slid out the comms device tucked into
their legrandian point, nestled perfectly
between his hole and his star mass.

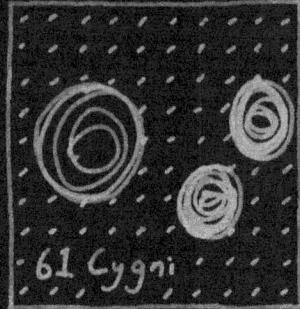

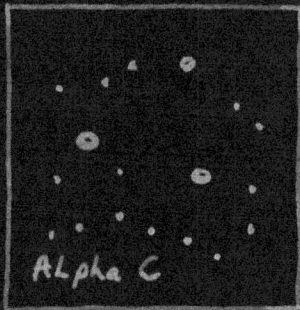

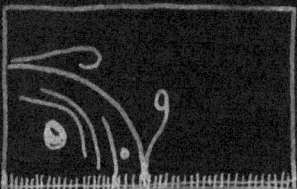

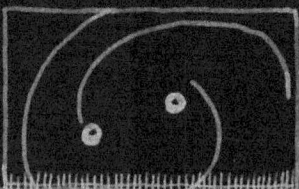

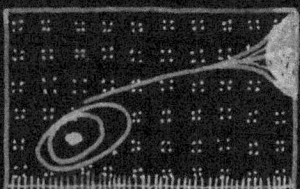

That's when E saw the profile, so dim it was almost inaudible. The mass so low that their lobes stood out at attention.

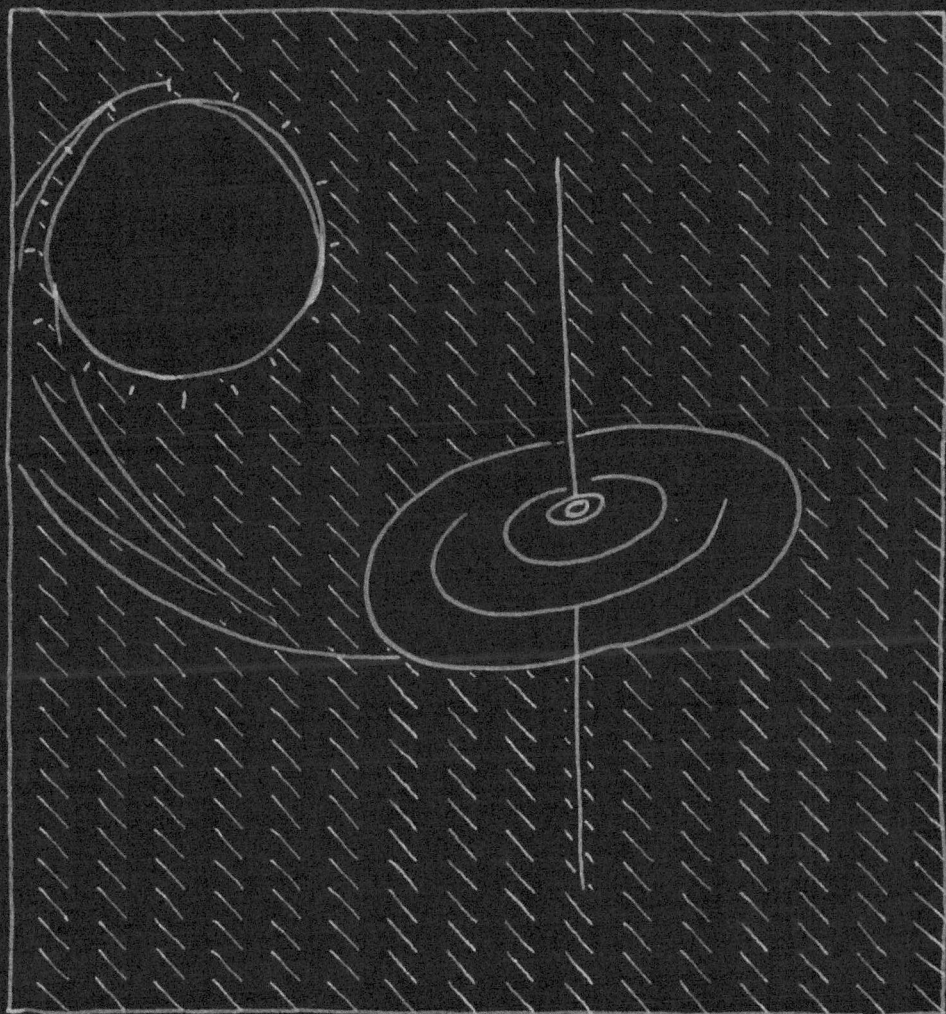

L cut a nebulus figure on the app's grid. Standing out by their quiet presence. A faint image amongst the firefly blue ionised thirst-traps E had become so accustomed to.

Are you on a different wavelength reading or is my photon reader in need of calibration?

No, nothing wrong with your reader.

I had a feeling...

E, what's that stand for? Enormous, Extragalactic, Eden?

E is for Eon, my parents had a strange sense of humor. FYI your lobes are exquisite...

I'm low-mass btw, means my lobes shine brighter than cis binary stars.

That even possible? You must be a rare one?

We are, but they find more of us every cycle.

Wanna meet?

Meanwhile, in a rarely stable solar
system on the orion arm of the milky
way. Dr Tana Joseph describes binary
star systems to a group of writers /
artists / poets in a valley nestled
between blue-stoned mountains.

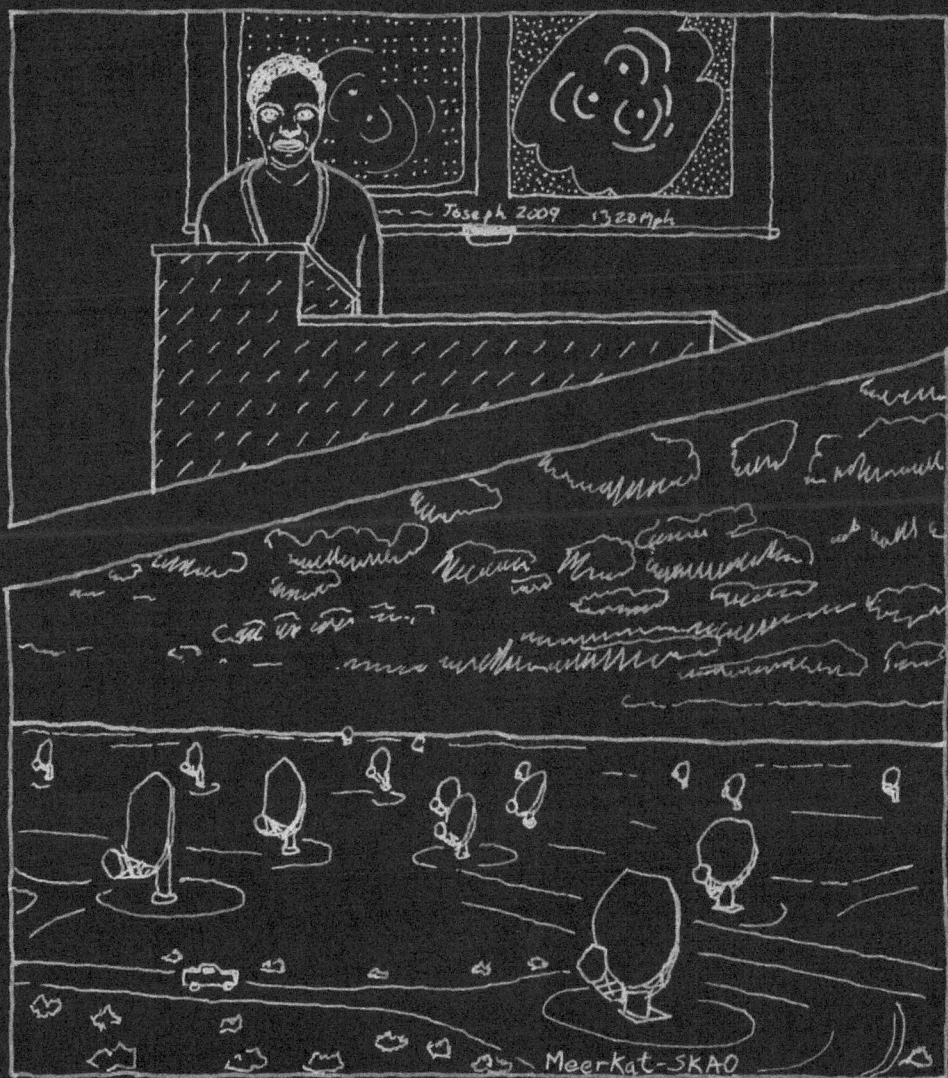

Two artists share a conversation en-route to their much-needed residency in Stellenbosch.

What a view.
Imagine living here...

The queer cliche of living
on a farm...

Really? I haven't heard that before.

A commune of queers living
on a farm together.

As a first generation non-farmer,
I'll definitely pass.

We can barely resolve normal
disagreements, imagine...

Maybe in a world where we weren't
brought up on ads, apps and 'amerigo'.

What does stellenbosch mean?

Probably some son of sorrow
named it after himself.

Now imagine the artist, a poet sitting in
this car, who absorbs all matter and
information during our residency.

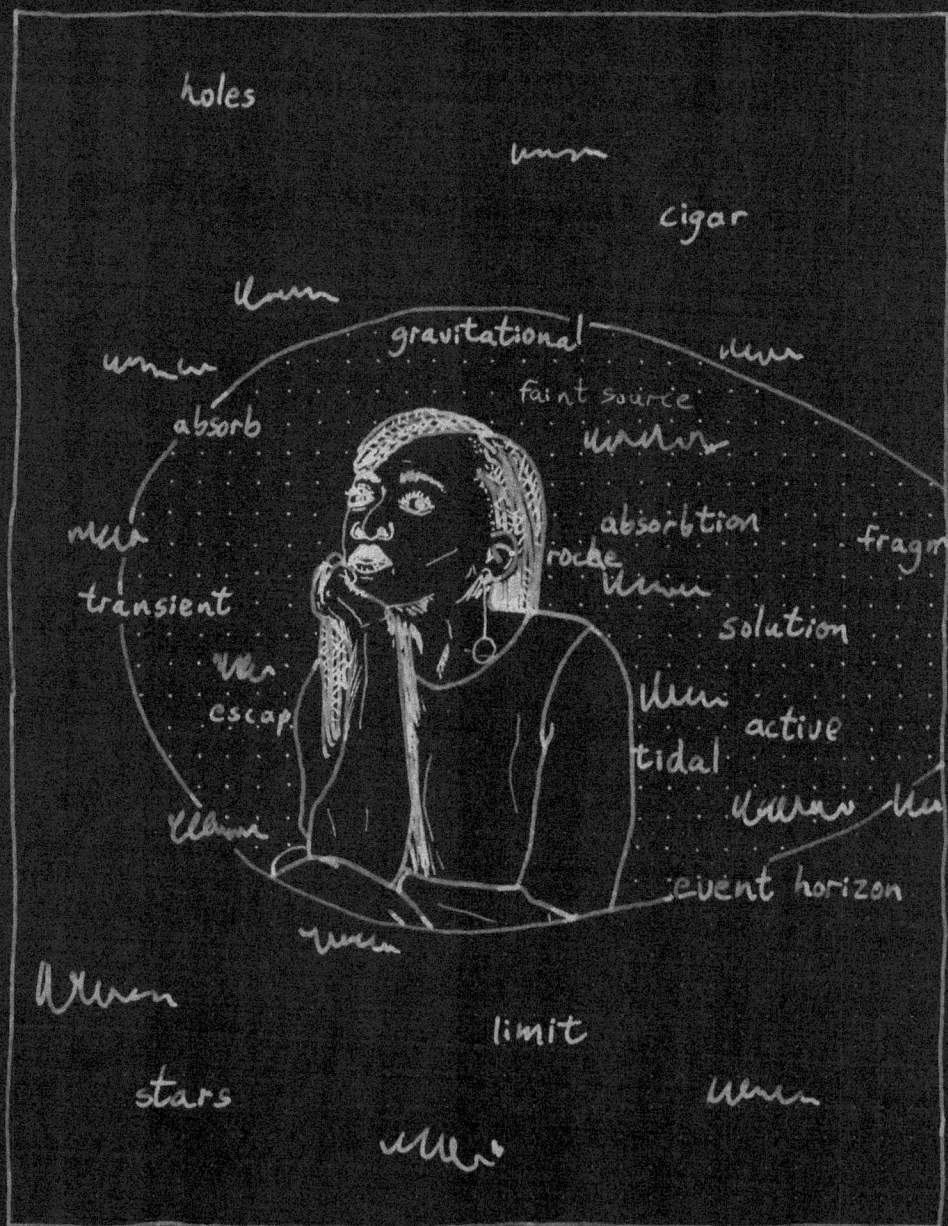

holes

ᶜᵘⁿᵐ

cigar

ᶜᵘⁿᵐ

gravitational

ᶜᵘⁿᵐ

faint source

ᵘⁿᵐ

absorb

ᵘⁿᵐᵘ

absorbtion

fragm

roche

solution

ᵐᵘⁿ

transient

ᵘⁿᵘ

escap

ᵘⁿᵘ

ᵘⁿᵐ

tidal

active

ᵘⁿᵘᵘ

event horizon

ᵘⁿᵘ

ᵘⁿᵘᵐ

limit

stars

ᵘⁿᵐ

ᵘⁿᵐ

They accrete references - unable to escape,
compressed ideas, an event horizon so
saturated with meaning that it collapses.

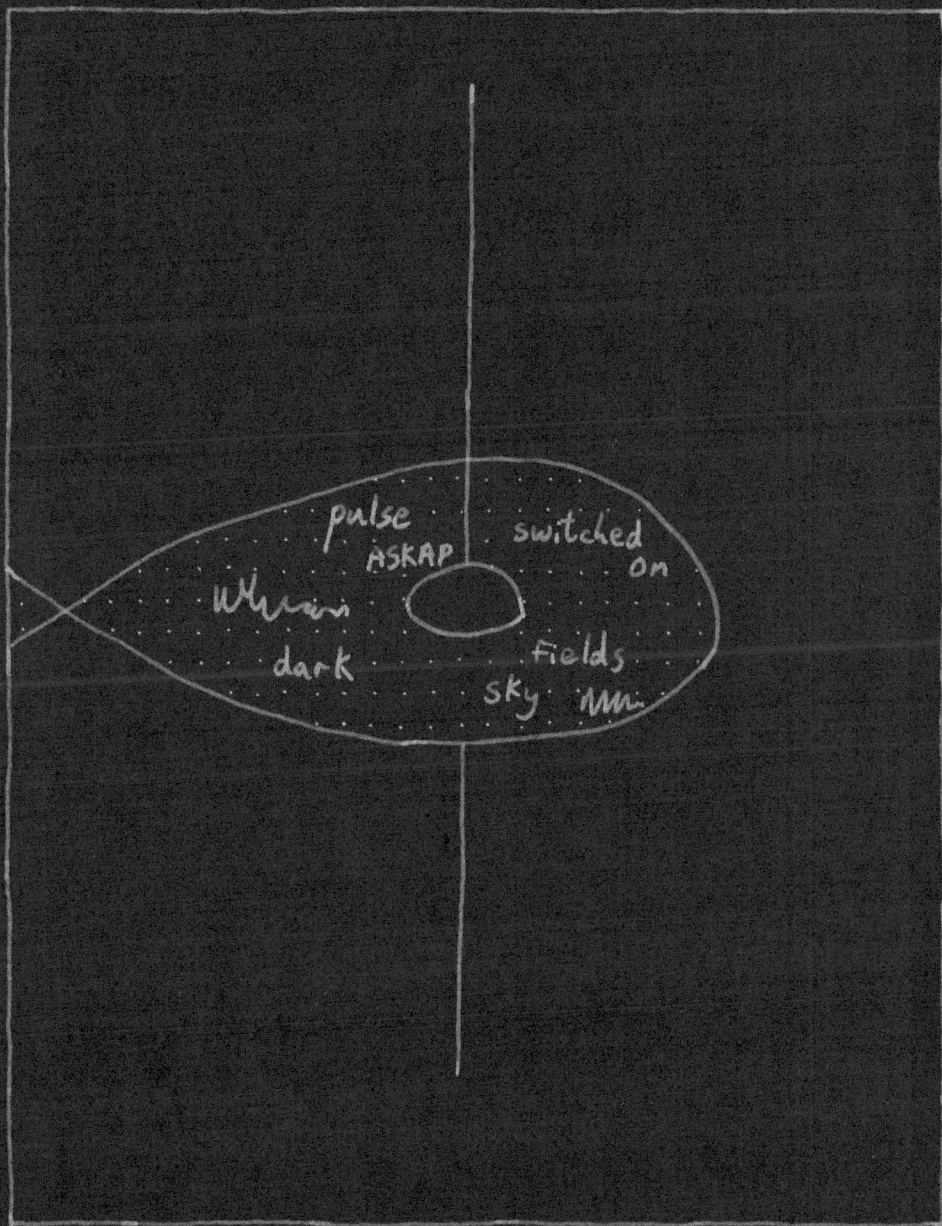

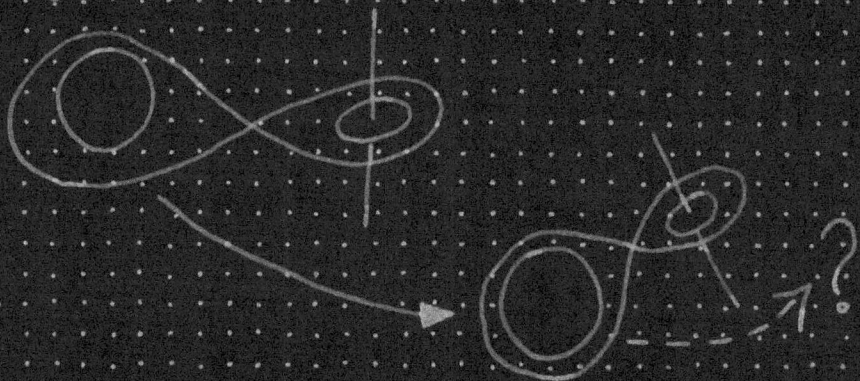

E & L take the plunge. They fall deeply into an interaction spiral with each other. Their merger outcome is unknown.

Artists/writers fall into exchange with each other between blue mountains. The words and their forms unwritten.

6

Three Poems

Mathapelo Mofokeng

Sky as Family Archive

Last night
I lay on the grass
to look at the sky.
It was blank
a cluster of stars cramped in my chest.

Ancient breasts swept supernovas under the circular grey rug.
Mama, a ram, has not spoken of
the bloody metallic taste left by *something* –
something to do with a father,
an uncle,
a magnetic field.

What occurs when lips sealed by gravity are left for fifteen minutes?

Peace.
Hypertension.
One suicide.
A Disappearance.
Ha re hopole, they claim.

What is the shape?
Volumes of pain.
A cigar.
A fried egg.
A hot blue, a cool red.

What does it become?
(The pitch of) A flock of birds ingested by an aeroplane's engine.

What is the assumption?

Power
Some other observing civilizations may say: Culture
How does it change?

I may burp the milky yellow gas into my palm,
watch silence crash, collide, wobble. It falls.
Words engulf each other. Truth stands –
tuck it safe into my bra.
Hand it down one day.

Not for the sake of a beautiful sky.

Sky as Metaphor

An admirer of poems
in two minds to reach uni-verse.
Today, my ego radiated heat,
did a breathtaking swirl,
replaced a giant star
after I finished *Sky as Family Archive.*

Despite my delight, I apologise.

Written from impulse,
reading it back, I see
a poem extractive in its formation.
Words drenched with sweat,
a crooked back,
a tired arm,
a galaxy cleared for an album.

The contemplative parts ask,
"Why have I written of the sky as symbol,
when binary stars and Magellanic Clouds are as real as whole?"

Sky as Endings

Halfway through life
a boy five billion years old
only Earth cries.

Dear donor
die, cool down, stop glowing
abandon your companion.

No one telescope
perceives the widows cloak.
Everlasting.
Beginning and all.

7

Sky Counsel

*by memory's daughter**

Nomhlaba dropped her head in her hands, slumped her shoulders and allowed the little girl within to release a whimper of overwhelm.

Her fingers picked at the resilient band between the 13th grey bead and the first white bead on her Menarche necklace. A thread of 27 beads, 4 white, 5 red and 18 grey—a gift from the elder sisters in her clan given at the ceremony marking her first bleed. As part of the ritual of tending to herself, every morning she'd move the band over one bead. It was a calendar for her bleed cycle: white for ovulation, red for her bleed and grey for the rest of the month.

As she moved the band back and forth, visions of herself and the slow, titillating lovemaking of the night before excited her vulva, still enlivened and nourished by the memories of pleasure.

From the beginning of This Time, the women in Nomhlaba's tribe had been guided by the knowledge, wisdom and understanding captured in the scrolls of MamKhulu. MamKhulu, the Great Mother, stretches across all that the eye can see in an indigo arch-shaped dome, her hands and feet placed firmly on either side of creation. Every day, MamKhulu begins the circadian labour of bringing the Sun God to life. The blood of this act stains the sky shades of red until the Sun God emerges fully formed in its rightful place. As night falls, MamKhulu consumes the sun and begins the work of birthing the stars and moon which swim across her belly and breast settling into their most familiar and comforting crooks and nooks of her body.

During the ceremony of their first bleed, girls are initiated into the knowledge of the Divine Feminine. Together the women learn and recite MamKhulu's words:

> From stellar-nurseries we come
> Amidst this swirling wind of gas and dust, stars are born.
> From this star-stuff humans are made.
> This is the origin of the iron in our blood, the calcium in our
>   bones.
> All of the mineral material of which we are composed.
> Binary Stars
> Tiny molecules of eternity perpetually seek companionship.
> Two stars bound to each other as the result of a fateful
>   event.
> We co-create a gravitational pull from which neither star
>   desires to, nor can, escape that leads to a dance of co-
>   evolution.
> This is the power of incarnating into a body that holds a
>   womb.
> To make life.
> To rest in the bosom of eternity where giving and receiving
>   are but two halves of the same Truth.
> Know this:
> Your body is your own to understand and utilise powerfully
>   for that which you have incarnated to do.
> May these beads, the moon, stars and sun empower us to
>   live autonomously.

With MamKhulu's ancient words looping in her mind, Nomhlaba scribbled the facts of her reality onto an empty page in her diary:

> "Oh MamKhulu!
> I've made love with a man.
> His sperm has entered me.

And the band of my Menarche necklace sits on a white bead.
An egg may have been fertilised; implantation may occur.
It is possible that as I sit here, I may be becoming pregnant.
Though my actions may say otherwise, I don't wish to
    mother a child now.
Most of all, I want this egg to be released and when the moon
    is full to *please bleed*."

Intuitively she moved her hands to her heart and began rubbing it, soothing herself as her elders had taught her to do when things became too much. Through the soothing sensation of self-care and touch, she returned to her body. Back from her imaginings of the implications of being with child and into the body over which she had dominion.

From this place of stillness she tuned in.

From somewhere and everywhere and nowhere at all, she heard/felt/smelled/saw a reply.

"Go back, my dear. Descend into the abyss. Find the
sleeping spirit of your culture and give it eyes. Look. See."

Vivid images of ancestors beamed into her vision from the distant past:

She saw groups of slave women rebelliously harvesting
    cotton root bark under cover of night.
She watched them as they chewed this bark as contraception
    and abortifacient.
Rebelling against their wombs' enlistment to producing
    another generation of slaves.
Images from even further back in time flashed into view. So
    far back, in fact, to be almost parallel to the present day,
    came into vision.
Images of women tending fields of white dwarf, *mhlonyane*,
    of blue and black cohosh, of don quai and wild carrot
    came into view.

Open air pharmacies intended to cater to the wellness and thriving health of women's bodies.

She took another deep breath here. Here in the sweet abundant solace of counsel.

With the next breath she opened her eyes and, borrowing resolve from the mountain that stood formidably in front of her, she straightened her back. She slipped on her Menarche necklace, gathered up her *muthi* pouch into which she slipped, *mpepho*, a perlemoen shell, filled a copper vial with water, wrapped her *umbhinqo* around her waist and set off up the trail.

Her destination was set. She was on her way to the diorite stone circles. The sacred space of medicine and initiation she had accessed throughout her life. Until this moment, all of her trips to this place had been in groups. Groups of families, of women, of community. Today, as she was told she would one day have to for reasons known only to her, she went alone.

She examined the sky.

"About two hours," she concluded her calculation aloud. "Perfect."

With a committed pace she'd arrive at the site just before the sun had set.

The journey was smooth. Her bare feet were familiar with the rocks and clay of this place. The certainty of her steps reverberated through her skin, blood, bones and all the other bits in between. This certainty in turn returned her confidence. Before she even decided to, she broke into song:

"Igama lamakhosikazi malibongwe!"

The three words of a song she'd sung all her life looped on repeat. And with each refrain the praise she dedicated to the names of woman was deepened until her own body began to shake ever so slightly with the praise she realised she herself deserved.

"Umzimba wamakhosikazi mawubongwe!" Slightly taken aback she realised that she had unconsciously infused the traditional song with her current state of mind.

Finding a rock smooth enough to perch on, she paused for a short break, took a sip of water and jotted down the realisation that had shot into her mind like a flare of consciousness.

She scratched in her pouch for her notebook and carefully captured the songline she'd just caught:

It is our bodies.
Our bodies too must be praised.
We are not abstractions.
Our bodies are vessels of the *materia prima* of the
multiverses.

Restored and clear-minded she allowed the mountain air to breathe her a few more times. She packed up her things and continued to climb until she arrived at a wide clearing on the side of the mountain. Installed into the landscape were the concentric stone circles from which her people had sought and received counsel for an eternity, before the words she spoke existed.

The simple act of arriving. The certainty and comfort of having somewhere to go with burdens too heavy to bear was already a resolution.

She cast her eyes to the horizon and calculated that she had just under an hour to catch the setting sun. With gratitude in her heart for a safe journey, she began, as she had been taught, to tend to the sacred work of ceremony.

Sitting in the centre of the circle she carefully removed the leaves from the dried *mpepho* bush she had travelled with and rolled them into a ball which she placed on her perlemoen shell. She poured spring water into a copper bowl as offering. Lighting the sacred fire she began her incantation:

"I call all my well ancestors to draw near to hear and hold
safe, healing space for my journey.
I call for help, resourcing and guidance.
To all of you, and myself, too, I ask to be led to ancient
knowledge of how to help my body release an egg instead
of implanting it."

She disrobed and lay naked at the centre of the circle flat on her back. She spread her legs and arms wide in the direction of the cardinal points. And, in time, her vulva caught and soaked up the elemental medicine of the setting sun. This she had been taught as a girl at her Menarche Ceremony. The rays of the setting sun provide medicine your vulva intelligently knows exactly how to use. Today, it wept nectar of excretion, ecstasy and consequence. And she, in solidarity, shed tears alongside it.

In the swirling cauldron of her most sincere prayer, her bodily pleasure remembered, reinforced by the thousand lapping tongues of the setting sun's rays, the swirling smoke of *mpepho*, and the majesty of the sky reflected on the water in the copper vessel, she journeyed beyond the physical world.

As she emerged on the other side—in The World Between Ours and The Next—she became conscious of clay-covered women surrounding her and daubing her own body with clay. She felt her body grow roots into the earth. When she opened her eyes, she realised she was in the great embrace of MamKhulu.

"I came because you called my child," MamKhulu transmitted, crystal clear, across radio waves Nomhlaba's people had long-perfected the intuitive technology of tuning into.

MamKhulu was well-attuned to the distress of a young woman being acquainted with the thin line between pleasure and conse-quence, submission and boundaries, and how one develops the courage to act and create in alignment with that which one chooses.

MamKhulu's body turned a darker shade of her already dark blue. As her shades darkened, wisps of night clouds came into view and caught Nomhlaba's attention.

"My child," MamKhulu continued, "What is created cannot be uncreated. It must be transformed. Because you seek I will grant you the vision of *isiHuhwa*. This will magnify your own perception as if your own eye were eight metres wide. More importantly, it gives the viewer the gift of resolve. That which is unseen will become exquisitely apparent." MamKhulu's words reverberated across eternity.

"Vulva. Yoni. Mamush. Cookie. Cunt. Poes. Vagina."

Nomhlaba chanted the words she had learnt to name the sacred gateway. With each word she made energetic offering to the ancestral grief and bliss each term carried.

IsiHuhwa took hold of her vision and with it her attention was drawn in by the scarlet glow of the Small Magellanic Cloud.

"Blood!" Her psyche exclaimed. How fitting that hydrogen, the mineral basis of life force, should be the same colour as blood.

She scrutinised the source more intimately, enthralled by these heavenly compositions that so closely mimicked earlier universes that they serve as our best insight into how things came to be.

"Write this down my child," MamKhulu instructed her. Nomhlaba committed MamKhulu's lesson to memory:

> The presence of choice is the evidence of the evolution of
>   consciousness.
> Magellanic Clouds chaotically begin accretion before the
>   supernova remnants are settled.
> They offer themselves while still embroiled in the
>   maelstrom of becoming.
> Both eventualities exist.
> And so both are valid.
> Choose.
> To evolve is to broaden choice.

Nomhlaba had retrieved the first dosage of medicine and knew what had to be done.

Aloud she began affirming her choice decisively:

> "To the consciousness orbiting me, seeking embodiment
> and the experience of transforming from spirit into
> form, I greet and acknowledge your bold and honourable
> curiosity. I am humbled that you would consider my
> womb and my lineage as the conduit through which to
> have this experience of physical life on earth. Thank you."

She paused to allow these words and their implications to settle where they needed to in her body.

MamKhulu placed her hands, fingers almost touching, as they faced each other over Nomhlaba's abdomen. Comforted by the warm sensation of loving touch, Nomhlaba continued:

> "I see you and acknowledge your infinite potential and
>   incandescent light.
> I am not her.
> I am not the one you seek.
> This womb won't hold you.
> Not now.
> I relish in the possibility of a later union.
> For now, please bleed."

On this command, MamKhulu's hands began circling anti-clockwise over Nomhlaba's belly, the movement she had been taught energetically encourages expulsion.

"So it is," she affirmed with MamKhulu, returning the vision of *isiHuhwa*.

Nomhlaba emerged from The World Between Ours and The Next just as MamKhulu was birthing the sun and the trails of her birth fluid washed the sky red. She gathered her *umbhinqo* and tied it securely under her arms binding and securing her body in the way she had been taught by her sisters, the Northern Lights on the other side of the great ocean.

MamKhulu gave one last instruction: "Find the White Dwarf. Imbibed, the White Dwarf will bring the Red you seek. Let your sacred yes be your guide to creation in your lifetime. Cherish it. It is your infallible blueprint to a life of bliss and freedom."

Nomhlaba was jolted into consciousness as she remembered the vision of her ancestors she had received the day before as her journey began. The women in the field tending open air pharmacies, restoring themselves through their relationship with the earth.

Nomhlaba knelt in the posture of submission and rested her forehead on the floor. Her arms next to her legs, palms facing up, she prayed in gratitude for the counsel:

"In honour of and respect for the ancestral guard that kept
     watch all night, the heavenly forces that attended me and
     to myself,
To the divine dispeller of darkness and confusion that
     resides within me,
I bow in reverence and awe."

With that Nomhlaba closed the sacred ceremonial circle.

She prepared her excursion to the White Dwarf confidently
because she knew exactly where to find this plant that her clan
knew so well. Cotton root bark it was also called. A plant ally that
grew perennially in the wild as a shrub.

She made her way back down the mountain taking the path that
would lead her to the river and the thicket of cotton shrubs that
abound in the area. She greeted the plant reverently and gently
brushed her hand across the recently burst flower capsule that
exposed the cotton from its seed cocoon, indicating her willingness
to listen to and learn from the plant.

"How could we have forgotten?" a stunned Nomhlaba asked the
White Dwarf.

"Perhaps, your fixated preference towards tidy and uniform
assumptions led you down a completely false path. Once on that
path you became ensnared by fear and self-preservation, and you
couldn't source the courage to acknowledge that you'd based your
calculations on false assumptions. I've been here waiting for your
return; waiting for you to re-member yourself as the women you
saw in your visions. Despair and grit were your guides—the binary
impetus that allowed you to descend deep enough into the unknown
to find that which must be retrieved and emerge with new eyes," the
White Dwarf transmitted.

"*Yimi*," Nomhlaba declared to the White Dwarf.

"I will live in alignment with the consequences of what I have
seen asks of me. I will do good work well. *Yithi*. It is us who will remember and make our lives and our potency reverberate across
multiverses yet unknown," she clarified.

"Then take my bark root. Chew it for the rest of your white and grey days. Eat cow's liver and *morogo* frequently. You will bleed. Now go and begin the work of turning your vision into sights beautiful to behold," the White Dwarf instructed.

Two weeks passed.

On the morning of the 28th day, the day of the first red bead, Nomhlaba woke up just before dawn.

She squatted over the seedlings of her budding nursery and bled directly into the earth—onto and into the crop of remembrance of autonomy through living, thriving culture.

"Yithi," she stated encouragingly to her seedlings and those who tended to them alongside her.

"It is us."

---

* *The use of a pseudonym is an attempt by the writer to acknowledge the collective ownership of these ideas and wisdoms. That said, to pluck these ideas from the ephemeral, filter them through one's own body, mind, psyche and spirit, and emerge on the other side able to transmute these intuitions into accessible clarity and direction is the work of formidable and altruistic human beings.*

The people who have served as these orientating beacons in my night sky have to be acknowledged by name:

To Rachelle Garcia Seliga, the Northern Light. All of the medicine I share is because you attuned my vision to be able to better see, feel and understand all that was around and in me.

With reference to specific content I acknowledge the work of Samantha Zipporah, a herbalist, educator, citizen scientist, anarchist and witch. This story pays homage to her Zine titled "Please Bleed" (2020).

Finally, to you the reader, I acknowledge and honour the sacred journey you are on that has taken you for now, to my words. May they serve you in your errantry.

8

UMakhwezana

Peggy Tunyiswa

UMakhwezana sisizukulwana senzonzobila. Lowo wazal'uMakhwezana akazange wabonwa ngabasaphilayo nangookhokho babo. Ukhule enguzimele geqe, engenabahlobo nazihlobo. Ukhule esitya, ondlekile kodwa engazange wondliwa ngumzali okanye isalamane. Wayezondla ngento yonke ekhe yasondela kuye. Wayengenamkhethe nantandokazi kwizinto awayezitya, wayelwabelela nje yena xa ifikile into ethi makatye. Ekumilele nokulwabela oko, etsho ngomlomokazi ohlal'unqekekile nomqal'omnyama ongenasiphelo.

UMakhwezana lo wayenelizwi. Ingelo lizwi nje, linomtsalane obizela ngawona mandla amangalisayo. Ungahambi wodwa nawo, uhamba nephangw' elingapheliyo setyile, oku komlingi. Ngokuko kwakhe yena uMakhwezana ngewayezibamba angakhamisi, angakhuphi kwalizwi, ngakumbi lakufik' eliphango. Wayezazi ukuba utya okokoko ngulo mlomo wakhe wawuhlel'uthe ng'a. Icebo yayikukuba azulise ngokudumzela, atsho ngesithukuthezi sengoma yelolo, umlibe wento. Yayimthuthuzela ixesha elide noko le ngonyana yakhe, akhe akwazi ukunyamezela iphango. Wade wanengoqekelela yobunewu-newu engqonge loo mlomo wakhe usisiqalo sobunzulu. Waziwa kanje ke uMakhwezana, nje ngomlwabeleli weento zonke, ubunzulu bakhe nobumnyama bakhe. Wayengathandeki kuba wayengathembeki. Ebengakuginya wena nelo qathana umsikele lona.

063

Mhla wasondel'ebantwini waginy' amakhwenkwana
ayeyokuzingela. Yayiligquba elimthumqwasi neliqaqadekileyo
lamakhwenkw'angevayo. InguGqadambekweni nabanakwabo,
ooYeyam, uKe, uLe namawele uXhwitha noZithaphulele. Kwakukho
uBawayo noNcuva ingabo abakhokele bonke oomaqhingana abo.
Ashiya ilali ngemva esiya kwihlathi lakwaSomjwi. Lihlathi eli
elalidume ngokoyikeka ngenxa yamashwa, imihlola nezihelegu.
Abantwana babengavumelekanga kulo. Kodwa ke ezi, zazingeva
ngakuxelelwa, zazisiva ngokubona.

OoGqada babehleli ke bengabokuqala kwisehlo, bakugqiba
bayisasaze indaba seyiqholwe nangobuxoki. Yayikwa ngabo ke
abeva ukudumzela kukaMakhwezana kuqala kunabanye. Beza
seyingathi bebethiyisele, beqajisela nokuba yekabani loo nto
bakuyifumana; bengayazi benjalo naloo nto bayileqayo.

Wavakala omnye ebuza, "Niyakuthini ukuba nguhili lo
simleqayo?" Wavakala omnye egqotsa ukubadlula bonke:
"Ngowam loo hili ukuba ndimbone kuqala!"; wath'omnye "Hayi,
ngowam tshi! Uviwe ndim kuqala ndathi mamelani"; nanko
nomnye: "Asoze kaloku ngoba ndim othe utsho kweliph'icala".
Wanyukela nomnye esithi, "Uyavuya! Ndim obethe zesivuke
siyozingela namhlanje, yeyam laa nto!". Yaba nguZithaphulele othi:
"Masike sixhwithelane ke. Elowo abambe loo nto ayiqhawulileyo."
Yangathi uzanayo kakuhle, bakhe bathula becinga loo mxhwithwa-
xhwithwano. Wath'uBawayo: "Nisalibele kukuxoxa? Mna
ndimkile!" Watsho ezifunqula naloo nteshana yakhe ngawona
mendu ukuleqa kuMakhwezana. Labe lilandela ilizwi likaNcuva
esindeka sisiqu sakhe esituku-tuku, ukubaleka kumsokolisa:
"Undithathele nam, tshomi!" Bafunquka bonke ngaxeshanye
beleqisa emva koBawayo.

Wabe sele kad'elambile ke yena uMakhwezana. Wabathi
bimbilili ngetham'elinye bengaqondanga, akwasala nentsente
yabo! Wawaginy'uMakhwezana amakhwenkwan'elali engazange
watya mntu ngaphambi koko, akazinika nethuba lokuwangcamla
okanye lokuwasizela. Kwaku ngekho kwanto awakhe wayiginya
wakhe wayihlanza. Kwakungekho ncasa wakhe wayiva
yakhe yamonyanyisa, navumba lakhe lamkhonyulukisa.

Wayengakrakrelwa, wayengaqhwethelwa, wayengomiwa, wayengatsarhwa—kwakungekho kwanto imehlelayo; wayeginya qha!

Kodwa ingathi ngalamini waginya isimanga. Waginy'abantwana babantu. Izintw'ezingaginywayo! Wabimbiliza ezazizelwe ngooQhashambula nooNongancama! Abazal'abangoo Phumasilwe kwabona, inimba isika okwendalo yayo! Babekhala bome, baphathe kuzibhuqa-bhuqa, befunisela ngabantwana babo. Bakhala zaliqela iintsuku, kwasala izingqala kodwa tu abantwana. Kulusizi nje. Umntu ngoku seyingathi yingonyama ukugquma sisingqala esixube nenqala! Phofu begquma nje, kungekho nto babenokuyenza ngaphandle kokwamkela ukuba iintsana zabo asoze ziphinde zibuye. Yenye yezinto awathi waziwa ngazo ezo uMakhwezana, ukuba waginy'amakhwenkwana eyokuzingela engamenzanga nto.

Ze yona engathethwayo ibeyindlela azisa ngayo uxolo nokuthula ebomini babantu. Hayi nje ngokuba waginya iinjubaqa zelali, kodwa ngokuhlalela kufuphi nabo wabaphumza kuSomjwi, isikhukhukazi semvula. USomjwi onebel'elid' elinye jwi. Lide lijikel'isifuba kathath' ukwehla ngesisu, ingono iyokuqondana ngqo nogqongo! USomjwi onwele lude kodw'aliwukhoth'umhlaba, luyaphila apha emva kwakhe xa ehamba okomsila wenja, wade walunika igama lokuba nguGala-gala kuba lumkhumbuza igala ngezimbo zalo. Olu nwele lwakhe lwaluyijoj'ingozi. Lwaluye lumxelele nangeendwendwe ezizayo. Njengamin'ithile amadoda elali azixelela ukuba imvula izakucelwa ngawo ekubeni yayiyinto yabafazi kuqala.

Ayesithi amadoda wona adiniwe kukuyifumana ngexesha labafazi imvula, elo siko lasekwa ngabangasekhoyo. Bona beyazi nje indlela eya eNtanabeni, ibotwe likaSomjwi, bazakuziyela. Batsho besithi isikhukhukazi semvula asinamkhethe, wonke umntu lintshontsho laso. Babezakusicenga ngezicengcelezo ezitsha nangeengom'ezahlukileyo, bezakubasipha izipho esiziqabukayo kodwa ezithandekayo. Bafunga bemunc'iintupha, bade bazinqakraza ukuqwela—ukuba izakuna nanini na beyifuna bona imvula, abanakufelwa yimfuyo neentsimi belind' amakhosikazi! Baya ke eNtanabeni besitsha benjalo.

Isikhukhukazi sasizihlele sifukam'imozulu. Azange sithande nakancinci sakuva ukuba kuza iindwendwe. Sasingaphazanyiswa ngexesha lemfukamo. Yayilixesha laso lokubumba imibethe, iimvula, izichotho, amakhephu nayo nayiphina into engamanzi ehla esibhakabhakeni ize emhlabeni. USomjwi xa efukamile, amaqand' akhe ebewakhusela kwiiMbobosi, izilo ezity'amanzi. Lali lixesha lakhe le ngcwangu eli la madoda ayesiza ngalo; umsindo wakhe wawuza msinya ngemfukamo.

Ayesondela kwelo botwe eshixiza ngaxeshanye, nyawonye, calanye, beman'ukuqakatha kanye ukubuy'umva naphambili bengathi ngumkhosi weembovane ufunqul'igqabi. Baqalisa ingonyana yabo yokuthuthuzel' isikhukhukazi, bade bayokufika phambi kwamasango ebotwe. Bacula bagqiba, bathula bezole. Balinda. Cwaka. Balinda. Nkcwe! Balinda. Bajonga ngapha nangapha bakuva kukhenkceza isandi esingathi seseentsimbi. Babhekisa emehlo phezulu kwezoondonga ziphakamileyo, akwehla nto. Bathi bakukhangela phantsi, nantso loo ngca ifuku-fuku babemi kuyo, isuke yama nkqo. Yamenyezela. Kwacaca ukuba ayongca nje, zizikhali! Abaphozisa maseko, bayiqala kwakhona ingoma yabo yokuthomalalisa ingcwangu yesikhukhukazi. Zangebaligqibe, babona kunyikima umhlaba, uqhekeka phakathi kwabo nebhotwe, kwavela umlambo phakathi kwabo neNtanaba ngesaquphe. Yangabo ngapha, iyiNtanaba phesheya komlambo. Bathi besothuke leyo, wathetha kwakanye uSomjwi wangcangcazelis' intaba.

Nangona la madoda ayengazange aliva ilizwi lakhe, kodwa alazi ukuba lilo eliya! Awazange adideke, athingaze okanye ayaluzele—aguquka ngelinye agqotsa ukuyikhomba emva ekhaya kwilali yawo yokuzalwa. Kwakungathi angacela umhlaba uwafunqule uwaphose ezindlini zawo, kuba isimo sasitshintsha esibhakabhakeni phezu kwabo besijongile. Amaf'amnyama aqokelelana ngephanyazo, engqubana kuthi gqekre imiban'emhlophe we kolo manyano lwawo. Abangabaleka la madoda ibe ngathi yilali ewabalekayo, kodwa engancami futhi engathothisi naloo mendu. Ilizwi likaSomjwi lisathi nkxwe ezindlebeni zawo, lisawarhiphule uvalo—indoda nganye

ixhina nentliziyo yay' esandleni ukugoduka. Bebhomboloza
amaxolo namatarhu. Watsho kanye nje uSomjwi wathi "Inzwi!"
Yana imvula yengqumbo kaSomjwi. Imvula eyayinamaqabaza
atshisayo okungathi kuneth'amalahle. Kowu! Yayimbi into! Owathi
wachatshazelwa yiloo mvula bekuphela nyi ngaye, athi nywam
abeliqabaza lokuginywa ngumhlaba. Nguloo mbono abahlali
abawubonayo ngaloo mini yokuqala kweNgqumba, imvula eyana
mhla ngengqumbo kaSomjwi.

Inyanga nenyanga yayisitsho loo mvula bezisola abayiqalayo.
Abahlali sebayiqhela bade bafunda nokuphila nayo.

Babesebelazi nexesha lokuza kwayo ukuba kubasemva
kwemini. Belwazi nohlobo lwamafu aza nayo, nokuba iyakuqabuka
emva kwethuba elingakanani na. Ubomi babahlali baguquka;
bafunda iindlela zokuzikhusela koko kutshabalalisa kwayo;
izindlu zabo zakhiwa ngendlela yokuba ze bakwazi ukungena
kuzo nakweliphi icala abeza ngakulo xa ehlanganisa loo mafu
akhawulezayo. Baqeqesha abantwana nemfuyo ukubaleka
ngolona hlobo xa lisiza elizulu. Noxa yayisaziwa ukuba iyakufika
emva kwenyanga futhi emva kwemini, eyona yure nomzuzu
zazingachanwa tu ke zona.

Phaya eNtanabeni kanti noSomjwi wayexakene nesiqu sakhe,
into kudala yammonqela. Naye wayengazange wavukelwa
ngumsindo kuba akazange wafumana sizathu sangqumbo.
Yayimxake kakhulu le yeNgqumba, engenako nokuncokola ngayo
ukuze afumane ingcebiso. Wayesithi seleseleseba kwelo bhotwe
lakhe, kuxwebe izityalo. Laa mini yamshiya edakumbile. umlomo
wawusel'unuka kukubunjwa, inye qha imini yokonwaba kuye: xa
abafazi bezokucela imvula. Wayeqale ewaqalekis'amadoda, wade
wayeka. Wayekhangela isisombululo qha. Kwade ke kwangaloo mini
eva ngay' uMakhwezana esenza esakhe isandi esingaqhelekanga.
Mhl'eginy'amakhwenkwana elali. Ngaloo mini wakhawuleza
wayazi ukuba akayedwa emhlabeni ngesiphiwo esingumnqa.
NeGala-gala lathi nta ukuma okwegala lothe ilanga, lingqina ubukho
besiqu esinefuthe langaphandle. Yavuy'inkodekazi, yatyhileka
ubuso ngomzuzwana nje. Yafunquka yalandela isandi, incediswa
nalunwele lwayo ukujoja elo cala lehlathi lalino Makhwezana.

Uchule kuhle ezizobela incoko ukuba ingahamba njani nondwendwe olo, evuyela ukuba lufike kakuhle engafukamanga. Wayedavaza nje pholileyo kodwa wakhawuleza weva ukuba lalikhona ifuthe elimfunqulayo, limbizela kulo. Wee khwashululu kwelokuyolelwa, wema ngxi ukuze abone ukuba nyani uyathatheka okanye uyazihambela na. Waweva kakuhle amandla elofuthe efika okwamaza echwetheza ingono nogqongo wakhe. Waqonda ukuba makaxhobe ngalaa Ngqumba kuba le aya kuyo ingayintanga yakhe nangaphezulu.

Wayeselekufuphi ukuba angasebeza aviwe nguMakhwezana, kodwa ekude ngokwaneleyo ukuba angaginyeki akusondela. UMakhwezana naye waziva izingqi, ifuthe nevumba elalikhokela uSomjwi. Waxakwa kukuba ngumfutho obuqheleka lowo kuye nangona engawazi. Wasuke wathiwa merhe ngumbilini, wawugunya ngoko nangoko. Wakhangela kwicala likaSomjwi, zagagana.

Nanko ethetha uSomjwi kungatshabalali nto. Aye esondela ngokusondela kuMakhwezana, engabizeleki futhi engaginyeki. Loo mafu entshabalalo ayengafumani thuba lakuqokelelana. Ayethululeka entubululu ukuya kuloo mqalakazi umnyama kaMakhwezana. Wayeziginya iiNgqumba zisaqala nje ukuphuma emlonyeni kaSomjwi. Loo nto yalenza ilizwi likaSomjwi lathamba, alabinabungozi. Nabo ubungozi bokubimbiliza kukaMakhwezana ababinabuhlungu ebantwini kuba engatyi nto yamntu.

Wehla uSomjwi ukuya ebantwini eyokuthetha nabo. Wabazisa ngoMakhwezana umzukulwana wenzonzobila. Hayi ke abantu bona, bathi nangona bebubona ubuhle bobuso bakhe, loo ntlaninge yamakhwezi neenkwenkwezi ezingqonge umlomo wakhe; bakhalima ngobumnyama nobunzulu bomqala wakhe. Bathi besiva ngamandla anawo, babe belilisela ngeenjubaqa awaziginyayobengayiva eyobuninzi beengqumba aziginyileyo, nokuba ngobukho bakhe phakathi kwabo asoze batshatyalaliswe kukuthetha kukaSomjwi.

Wabathembisa ukuba ukususela loo mini yena uyakuhlala encokolela uMakhwezana ukuze ingqumba ibesesona sondlo sakhe. Uyakuyinisa imvula ngokwaneleyo ukuze abantu nemfuyo

yabo bangalambi kwaye banganxanwa. Uyakuyinisa ngamadla
ngexesha lokucelwa kwemvula ngabafazi kuba yayiyimpilo kubo
ukusebenza ngamanzi. Kwavunyelwana, kwagqitywa. Babe ubomi
buyiloo mvumelwano ebantwini, kuSomjwi noMakhwezana.

Tyum. Tywabash.

Four Poems

Melissa Sussens

Space Teaches Survival

The lifetime of the donor star determines the lifetime of the binary,
names them both as having existed.

The smallest stars are the sturdiest. Survivors
despite all the lonely orbits, despite
the insatiable burn to belong
somewhere—beyond all those failed
first dates, the friendships that never
were. Light years of galaxy spent searching
for connection, longing to be held
by the gravity of another.
Existing on the other side
of hours spent cataloguing
the not-good-enoughs.

The bigger the star the faster it will burn
out. Collapse into supernova
inevitable. Neutron star or black

hole the only fate. These are just the facts.
And yet they are a manifesto
for those of us living outside
the binary, on the margins, in the orbit
of the (spot)light—

the queers afraid to name their love
in public spaces. The mothers
unable to speak aloud the loss of self
that follows new life. The desperate
dreamers unable to live
on their creativity alone. The donors,
the choiceless, those slaving
to others' desires.

Even the smallest
dots of luminescence
matter in the expansion
of the universe. Globular clusters tell
the ancient story of light years, space
measured by continued existence.
A group of small stars all born
together, their epoch a tale
to be told to us by the sky—
survival   equals   light.

The Donor Star Discovers Her Voice

You take everything
I have to offer,

or maybe I give
you everything I have. Unmake

myself so that you
can shine. Dim

my light, unmatter
my matter. You hold me

hostage in your glorious orbit. Our dance
an evolution that relies on this game,

old as the universe—in a binary
bind there must always be one

who will sacrifice. Fifty-fifty
a myth. No marriage can be

so simple. I know this, and yet
even depleted I will outlive

you. Will rename myself
the star that survived.

The Black Hole Takes the Spotlight

I cannot control the forces that make me
        what I am. I was born from collapse.
                Do not remember my ancestry
                        as supernova, or the time before
                that when I was star, glowing ball of matter
        and light. I know only to
absorb all that touches me. Energy
        cannot be created or destroyed
                but it can be swallowed. Warped
                      into something
                scientists cannot calculate—
        space and time different
for me. I travel without moving. Engulf
        entire worlds and their histories. I am the final
                destination of everything. Life cannot help
                      but be drawn to me. My gravitational
        pull exceeds
    all mass combined. Everything
is small, compared to me. A meal.
        No messengers come from within.
                Nothing to spill my secrets.
                      I do not allow even light to escape.
                It's safer this way. Protected.
        I am guarded by my own
penchant for destruction.
        I am every great apocalypse
                combined. I am
                      what comes after
                the nightmare. And yet,
        you cannot look away.

The Sun Mourns Itself

I am not special. Small. One
in a million-trillion like me.
No one can look at me,
I have never been held.
My flaming skin surface flares
away all potential suitors with its brutal
burn barrier. Their lives depend
on me. A system, I am
at the centre of. Important.
God-like, I can only be loved
from afar. Untouchable. Orbited.
Worshipped—never known.

One day I will expand, a reverse
melting to consume
everything in my system,
leave just a speck in a galaxy among
a trillion other dust dots. It will not matter.

Matter cannot be destroyed,
only transferred—the life-giving
energy of me floating out in pulse waves
will become something new. My planets
will die. There will be none I loved
to hold my wake. My embers
will dissolve in unmemory. The dead
cannot mourn and so I will be

unmournable. I will die as I live—alone
at the centre of it all. With softness, a slow
expansion and then
collapse. A turning
within, as I consume them all.
Eventually, even my own light
will not be left
to mark us as once here.

10

Planisphærium Coeleste

Skye Ayla Mallac

When viewed from above, the storm turned disparate and tranquil. Swirling sand coiled into a column and bisected the sky. And from the safety of their airship, suspended in a belly of wood, an assembly of scientists, air crew, and the wealthy son of a merchant watched as their planetary resources spun skyward and beyond.

It had begun with the metals, fifty years before.

Pulled like liquid threads from the rock, pooling onto the paving stones and then vanishing without a trace. The children noticed it first and tried to pry the hardened rivulets of silver and lead and copper and gold from their street corners, to no avail. Their fingers came away bloody and caked in grime.

The miners were the next to realise. The veins which they had tapped for decades, coaxing ore from the caverns of the mountains, were vanishing before their eyes. At first they thought the consequences of years spent in the oppressive darkness and cloying damp of their tunnels had clouded their senses. But then news came from across the country. There was no iron ore to be chipped free of the stone, no veins of gold were threading the rock, no nuggets of zinc left to be spat forth from the soil.

So the mines dried up and the people turned to other resources, oil and gas, wood and water, which might sustain their necessities.

And then the sandstorm came.

A great, swirling squall which swept across the landscape. Sucked forth by some sort of inexorable force. Shunting people from its path, causing settlements to flee to the harsh borders of a tempest which raged on, eastwards and upwards.

Eastwards, across the mountains whose peaks rubbed away to blunt nubs as the sandstorms picked more fodder from their flanks. Upwards, coalescing into a swirling stream high above the raging tempest which battered the earth below. Where it dulled the sunrise and the people who had fled to the borders of the ceaseless storm spent their mornings in muddied darkness.

It did not obscure the western sky, however, and its irrevocable eastward trajectory posed as much a mystery as the storm itself.

For the first few years every scientist was summoned to bring clarity to the inexplicable circumstance of the storm. But none came. The geologists watched their stones erode in loops and whorls, then disappear entirely, powerless to stop it. The physicists collapsed in incomprehension. The botanists watched vital species shrivel and die. Only the water remained unchanged, seeping through the eroding rock and gushing, clear and cold, down the mountainsides.

Years went by and the great ochre sandstorm became a fixture to the people. Onto whose maps the treacherous path of the tempest was marked as a permanent addition to the landscape. People were born, lived and died without ever seeing the eastern sky unclouded.

And eventually there came a time when any questions about the source of the perpetual storm were met with insouciance. It became difficult to imagine a skyscape that was wholly clear and blue. The mountains shrank, grain by grain, the deserts that lay in the path of squall emptied, and the people clung to what resources remained. Timber felled from dwindling forests, fresh water spat forth from the valleys of the shrinking mountains, food coaxed from soils which grew more barren every year, as trace minerals wriggled to the surface and broke free to join the inexorable aerial flow.

The world shifted to accommodate it. The people blinkered their view to the east and found comfort and continuity in the western skies.

After a time, only the astronomers continued their study of the sandstorm phenomenon, certain that it had something to do with the stars. Fuelled by a vague notion, driven by swift advancements in the study of electromagnetic particles, centred around an interplay of atmospheric physics, planetary dynamics, and celestial interactions.

But the ever-changing heavens, which they had once mapped into their Planisphærium Coeleste, their guide to the heavenly plane, with such ephemeral dedication, yielded no secrets. Their telescopes, great mechanical eyes ever-trained on the heavens, found it increasingly difficult to penetrate the haze which obscured the eastern skies.

And yet, with tireless commitment, they watched and they cal-culated, assumed and hypothesised, tying down the known skies—such as they were—with paper and ink and the unwavering hope that meaning might be gleaned from where there appeared to be none.

As their questions grew, minds trapped behind telescopes and equations, the world around them progressed and, in a town six days' travel from the Astral Observatory, a group of intellects and engineers tapped a bubble of buoyant gas and designed a ship that revolutionised air travel.

Within a year, the sandstorm was circumnavigated.

Where it had once posed an impenetrable barrier that covered the bulk of the continent, the journey could now be made in a matter of weeks. Cities, which had for so long been separated by the perennial squall, were connected once again.

And it is at this point that Cygnus Vega found his way to the doorstep of the Astral Observatory with a proposal in hand.

Vega was the son of a merchant who had risen to wealth within the space of two years through cultivating a roaring trade moving tea and spice around the sandstorm. He was fastidiously ambitious and had long harboured a fascination with the sandstorm, fuelled by a private desire to bring clarity to the mystery. While it was a fascination that spilled over into his life with frantic abandon, his father's recent rise to repute left Cygnus fiercely determined to carve out a legacy of his own, independent of his family's successes.

A year of committed work alongside his father had recently earned him his own airship and crew, and he intended to put them to use in a way quite unlike any would have expected.

Which found him one afternoon, face pressed in rapturous delight to the eyepiece of the Astral Observatory telescope, as a group of astronomers poured over his proposition.

He planned, he informed them, to sail west and then push the ship into altitudes that, while the ships had been designed to withstand them, had never been breached before. The intention, first, was to put enough distance between themselves and the sand-stream so as to observe it from a wide angle lens, such as it was.

The astronomers were hesitant. Having spent the entirety of their prolonged studies with their feet planted firmly on the ground, coaxing meaning from the lenses of their telescopes, the prospect of leaving the comforting confines of their wood-panelled halls and taking flight into the unknown was overwhelmingly daunting.

But Cygnus was obdurate in his thirst for discovery, and passionately committed to his course. And his enthusiasm was infectious. Within hours he had rallied a handful of scientists, lured them from the depths of their Observatory with the beguiling promise of informational boundaries breached, and had secured himself a crew of scholars who, he astutely hoped, would be able to sketch an understanding of the mystery once they had uncovered it.

For, he was sure, they would certainly uncover it.

And so, with nothing but their Planisphærium Coeleste to guide their voyage, this company of astronomers, cartographers, wealthy amateurs, and a resigned crew of sailors set forth for altitudes and lands uncharted.

They sailed westwards for weeks, high above the barren landscape and the softening mountains. Westwards, across the inland sea whose waters sat eerily still as they had for decades. Westwards, and beneath them dying forests stretched their brittle fingertips towards the sky.

Behind them the sandstorm shrank infinitesimally every day. The ruddy horizon, so familiar, contracted and the sand-stream began to manifest itself into a column from this vantage point. The astronomers gazed and calculated, watched and hypothesised, and every day some miniscule change shifted their assumptions. And on they sailed, westwards.

After five weeks, by which time the sand-stream was clearly discernible as a towering pillar sweeping heavenward, Cygnus announced it was time to begin their ascent. It would be a gradual one, allowing them to acclimatise to the thin air and icy conditions. This shift was just as minute as their slow retreat from the sand-stream itself. So gradual it could hardly be perceived, decibel by decibel, and then all at once, the perspective shifted.

It happened in the dead of night. A scream from the stern woke the crew with a start and within minutes Cygnus and the astronomers were roused by trembling sailors, beckoning them with wild eyes that betrayed, not fear somehow, but crippling awe.

They scrambled to the viewing deck and felt the breath knocked out of them as if by physical force.

Before them, years away and yet before them, the ochre stream of sand was whipped into a centrifugal whirlpool. A great river of vermillion spun, disc-like, faster and faster and faster until, in one blinding moment where a velocity that surpassed imaginable parameters was reached, this matter shot out lengthways along the axis of the maelstrom and an astrophysical jet perforated the sky.

A crow of understanding broke from the throat of one of the astronomers but she could find no words for this sudden rush of comprehension. Her heart swelled within her chest until it all but stopped her breath. This intricate circumbinary interaction between their own planet and the fiery dead star around which they orbited was searing. Understanding shot through her as she watched the stream of the sandstorm, pulled irrevocably on by the irresistible magnetic force of a neighbouring celestial body.

She sank to her knees alongside the rest of the crew, struck dumb by the whirling phenomenon unfolding before them.

But something was wrong. The great craft shuddered, and a rallying cry of alarm rose from the sailors, shaken from their reverie. Hands leapt to their stations, the mechanical engine thrown into reverse and descent. But the forces at play were too strong.

Even from this distance, invisible gases were being sucked into the vortex, caught in the endless flow of matter leaching from their planet. Their own airship, held safely aloft by buoyant gas, betrayed them.

And with a great heave of wood and wind, this motley assembly of people whose lives had for so long been absorbed by the mystery at play was sucked irrevocably eastward and upward into the mystery itself.

Eastward and upward into the Planisphærium Coeleste.

And in this equivocal dance on the heavenly plane, the living planet fed the dead star and the dead star shone.

11

Look Up! Don't Look Up!

Mehita Iqani

iBall Launch

Teleprompter script
[AV directions added]

Strict embargo

[lights up]

[enter stage right]

[wait and look at camera for five seconds before speaking]

It's the next step in the evolution of human sight.

A chance to see further than ever, to see things never seen.

Ladies and gentlemen, theydies and gentletheys---

I am pleased to announce the launch of our latest
product---

[play approved_brand_intro01.mp3]

The iBall.

[play approved_brand_outro04.mp3]

For almost a century we've been making the best
communications devices. So much of our work has
helped human beings express themselves, connect
with loved ones across the planet, and see things
happening on the other side of town, the country,
and the world.

With all we've done to contribute to the
enhancement of human perception, turning our
attention to the business of perfecting the eye
was only inevitable.

For years now, R & D has been tirelessly
dedicated to inventing the best and biggest
eye possible with current technology. Today,
we reveal the first commercially available
application of our technology.

The iBall is the largest eye ever to exist. It
can see further up and out than has ever before
been possible.

Our patented connection device implements
decades' worth of artificial intelligence eye-
tracking technology, and lets you plug in
directly to see what the iBall sees.

But first, let me take a step back and show you
how it works.

[lights down, play iBall_install_intro.mp4]

As you folks can *see* (pun intended!), the iBall

is installed on the roof of your home. At eight
metres wide, of course it's only suitable for
homes of certain size and structural integrity.

Though we do imagine that in the future those
living in tighter quarters or more communal
arrangements will be able to purchase and install
their own iBall through collective credit
arrangements.

For now, though, for proprietary and maintenance
reasons, the iBall can only be purchased by
people with eight-metre - or more - diametrical
space available on their roofs.

Our iBall team will deliver and complete the
installation in less than a day. For the brain
hardware insertion, you'll only need to pop into
our iBallPark - no appointment necessary and we
guarantee no wait longer than 10 minutes.

The painless procedure should be over in a few
seconds. Once you're home, you can plug directly
into the iBall and observe the mysteries of the
universe all for yourselves.

[play galactic_vibration_05.mp3 on loop]

Although in the past we've worked to create
smaller and more compact products, when it comes
to seeing, bigger is better. We discovered that
the optimal size for a technical eyeball exten-
sion was eight metres in diameter.

This allows the iBall to see for light years
across space for you. Any less and you wouldn't
see much at all. Any more and your brain won't be
able to process the data.

Eight metres is the sweet spot for extending
human sight further into space.
There is no need to imagine the universe,

or strain to make out shapes on fuzzy radio
telescope mock-ups, to see that newly discovered
distant galaxy everyone is talking about. Simply
blink-scan in the universal coordinates.

Like a satellite, the iBall will turn in the
correct direction, and you will instantly see it
for yourself. Real space vision, in real time.

Thanks to the iBall, it's all right there within
your eyeshot.

As well as being able to see as far into space
as is possible with terra technology, the iBall
integrates all sorts of wave-detection ability.

It can see radio waves, microwaves, infrared
radiation, ultraviolet rays, x-rays and gamma
rays, as well as your ordinary optical waves,
RGB, that sort of thing.

There is no better way to look up, than with the
iBall.

Looking at relatively proximal features, like
your back garden, or the highway while you're
driving to work through the iBall, would be
blurry because they're too close to focus on with
an eye that big.

Life on this planet has evolved eyes that are
best adapted for seeing the things around us that
we need to see, like food sources, or whether
there is another vehicle moving slowly up ahead.

So when we want to look up and out, as we have
for centuries yearned to do, craning our heads,
straining necks, our measly little eyeballs are
not up to the task.
The iBall is specifically designed to see light
sources that are visible in the dark, obviously.
What to a regular human eye, only two centimetres

in diameter, just looks like a twinkly little
star, to our eyeball looks like---

It's indescribable. So let me show you these
reels from my view last night.

[play iBall_sights_reel_05.mp4]

Oh, the utter thrill of seeing swirling gas
clouds of hydrogen and helium!

Radiation plumes jetting out in a stream 5000
light years long!

The heavy bullet of black holes glaring through
the background!

All god's angels and armies gathered in gaseous
form!

The slow dance of universe expansion!

All this in real time and real space, from the
comfort of your home with your very own iBall.

If we had eight-metre wide eyes, we wouldn't
need to eat. We'd spend all our days fixed to the
earth, rooted, perhaps; the rest of our bodies
evolving into smaller appendages that grew into
the ground to absorb whatever nourishment was
needed to fulfil the function of nourishing the
eye.

The eye-brain, that would look up and up and up---

Until such a time, we have the iBall.

You can open your iBall just after dusk. It
should be pointed up, always up. We have designed
the eyeball so that it swivels no more than one-
eighty, so you can scan from horizon to horizon.

Because of this angle, the neck of the eyeball
must always be positioned in an upwards leaning
position. Ergonomical loungers are also available
for purchase from an iBallPark near you. An
integrated cable unit allows the viewer to plug
into their iBall from the most comfortable
position for looking up and out.

We are proud to offer this product as the state-
of-the-art solution to looking into the night
sky. This is something humans have always wanted,
and now it's within everyone's reach.

The sight is, literally, heavenly. To bring those
heavens closer: priceless.

I thank you for your attention.

Good night.

[play approved_brand_outro07.mp3]

[lights down]

[exit stage left]

Don't Look Up*

*

There are presidents that all the world knows, even though they are not our presidents, and constitutions and amendments that we cite even though they are not ours. There are people who want to ban abortion, who are doing so, and who want to force teachers to defend little kids from gunmen. Using guns. Here is a place built on slavery where Black Lives should Matter but still don't. There are red stripes, too, but here are fifty stars, white, lined up in unison against a blue background.

They sell the promise of free market capitalism no matter the cost.

*

Climate change apocalypse: it's only four degrees, people, calm down, keep pumping the petrol, keep burning the fuel to make the commodities, keep driving the cars to malls to buy them. The logo used to be a red five-point star in a black circle on a white background. Then, it was re-jigged by eager graphic designers into a white star on a teal and red background, a resolute red arrow extending from the left hand of the star into the red abyss of the future.

It lobbies and lies to pump more oil and pocket more profit.

*

This is the portrait of the famously handsome freedom fighter. He gazes sternly, sexily, into the future, resolute about the struggles ahead. His dark hair flicks around his face from under the military beret, one star at its centre. It seems to float like his third eye, his furrowed brow, seeing into the future.

It says, the people liberate themselves.

---

* Asterisks everywhere.
  Looking everywhere but the night sky,
  I see stars.

*

It is hot today, and the air quality index says it's safe to be outside. This is the sixth largest city square in the world, soaked once with the blood of anything from several hundred to several thousand people—because reports cannot be verified. One of whom stood slenderly in front of the tanks with his shopping bags, the meal ingredients inside never to reach home. A very large red flag hangs from a very tall pole, limp in the heat. If a wind was to pull it open, on its sea of red there we could see one large yellow star, here four smaller ones curving its eastern flank.

They sold the great leap forward.
They sell capitalism with socialist characteristics.

*

There on a shelf is a brand-new pair of white high-top sports shoes, with eight-eye laces and a bendy rubber sole. There is a price on the label. On the canvas, encased in a circle, a black star imprints the ankle.

It sells running and jumping and standing around
on the street looking cool.

*

There is a red carpet going up steps. There is a door, heavy, but it will be opened for you. Golden light glows from within. Someone will carry your bag after you check in, they will also show you to your room, explaining with some care how to switch on lights and the television. There will be too many pillows on the bed. The sheets will be soft, three-hundred thread count. There will be a robe in the wardrobe. There will be a minibar in the fridge. The drinks will cost more than they should. On a brass or brass-ish plaque at the entrance to this establishment, five stars will be arranged in a gentle curve, the middle one largest and highest.

It promises you a better home away from your
probably ordinary home.

*

The chain store used to sell engagement twin-set rings. The fancy floral or starlike arrangements of tiny diamonds on the first, most important, ring indicated the extravagance of the promise. The second, more modest ring was plainly moulded to match the shape of the first; its relative simplicity symbolising the drudgery, perhaps, of the years ahead once the party is over. The sets would be arranged on velvet display cases under glass counters, which were polished daily before opening time, and on which fluorescent lights would shine to accentuate the sparkle of the diamond chips. The sets could be purchased on credit arrangements which required the happy couple, or at least one of the two, to fill in detailed forms that disclosed income and the particulars of other retail accounts held. Now, the chain store has rebranded into an online-only outlet aimed at youthful customers looking for affordable, fashionable, decorative items—gold or gold-plated. The online stock list is inspired by "all things celestial"; its logo offers an eight-point star in place of an ampersand.

It used to sell romance; now it sells fun flirty independent femininity.

*

The first African nation to throw out the colonialists, the first leader to dream of African unity. A celebration of freedom from white rule. In the centre of a yellow stripe, bordered by red at the top, green at the bottom: there is one Black Star.

We face neither east nor west; we face forward.

*

You should strive to achieve this small marker. It says something about you, personally. It is nice to look at. It is a reward, sometimes accompanied by handwritten exclamations, such as "Great work!", "Keep it up!" and "Excellent!". In your exercise book, in the margins, is a small sticker. It is shiny. Sometimes it is put on your forehead instead.

You followed the rules and did what you were supposed to.
You are a good child.

*

If you're only attracted to people of the same sex, and you think that sexual desire is fixed, and you've never had a lover of a different sex either by choice or chance, then you might think of yourself as a gold star version of your kind.

Stereotypes upon stereotypes.

*

There is a single red star standing alone. To the right, a name is written in heavy, reassuring green letters. On a green bottle, the white outlined red star lets you know that it's time to take a break for the day.

This cold beer will make you funnier and more attractive.

*

There is a crescent moon, and next to it a star.

This is your faith; may peace be with you.

*

Two equilateral triangles lie on top of one another, pointing in opposite directions. Together, six points. In a black outline on yellow fabric, sewn onto your jacket, the star indicated that a genocidal maniac and a crazed society that enabled him decided that your living body should be starved then burned. They sent you away wearing it in a crowded train carriage, likely towards a horrific death-gas chamber. In blue outline on a white flag, this star symbolises the haven for your people, though you may or may not agree that this long-awaited homeland is built on a territory taken by force from others. If you ever go to Auschwitz, to pay respect to the six-million-plus murdered souls, to bear witness to the gouging and bloody arc of history, to remember and join a collective promise of never again, you might come across a group of Israeli youth. They might be praying, embracing each other, weeping. They might carry their flag around their shoulders.

Here is your synagogue; here is your nation.

*

There is a fish, a silver-blue pilchard. It is out of water. It seems justifiably concerned that there is no blue ocean in sight, only a red flatness decorated by thin yellow stripes. It seems that it is to be grilled. A bright yellow star, with additional starburst lacerations beaming from between its points, tells the fish it is lucky.

It sells Omega 3s.

*

There is another red star standing alone against a white background. To the right, a name in the possessive is written in delicate round black font. The apostrophe is replaced with a little black star.

They sell accumulation for its own sake.

*

A double barrier circle enshrines the claim. Inside, a map with the national flag fills the borders. The emblem has six stars embedded into the borders of the badge: three on one side, three on the other, and each one in the middle of the trio a little bigger than the other two.

They indicate that the item you're holding was made in your country.

*

Three faceted shafts radiate from a central area ending in sharp points, embedded in a wheel that looks like it might be ready to steer a vehicle.

It sells luxury individual transportation.

*

There is a silhouette of a mountain, in negative colour, white where the shadow should be, black for snow. A name bends over the top. In a perfect half circle, a couple dozen stars arc up and over, starting and ending at opposite bases of the hill, peaking above its summit.

It sells spectacle.

*

Five diagonal lines intersect and connect to form a five-pointed polygon. If you draw a circle around it and then turn the whole thing upside down, and dye your hair purple, and add some black make-up to your otherwise pretty face, you might upset the aunties at church. If you paint it on the ground and place a candle and a drop of menstrual blood in each corner, you might summon the devil.

It sells goth teenage rebellion.

*

They protect and serve. They bandy about their munitions to intimidate. They turn a blind eye. They take a long time to fill in forms that you will need for your insurance claim. They will keep you waiting if they don't like the look of you. Some of them will try, some of them will not. They know they are outnumbered by the criminals, yet they still must do this impossible job. Some of them are the actual criminals. On the uniform, is a badge. An eight-pointed rayed star with a slightly frilly texture holds a round blue band. Within that, sits an aloe plant with nine leaves and three red-hot-poker flowers in full bloom.

It promises emptily, as best it can supposedly,
to push back the frontiers of evil.

*

There is a feminine figure, her breasts coyly covered by long wavy hair, her lower body descending into a suggestive bifurcated fishtail. She wears a crown with a star in the middle.

She sells disposable cups of coffee.

*

Inside a lateral oval is a cluster of four-point stars, one larger on the upper left, five smaller to the right lower side. The Pleiades. It's just a logo for a very reliable car.

You can drive it to most places.

*

There is a stain on your white shirt that will only come out with some handwashing, and you need this green bar of soap for the job. Moisten the stained fabric, rub in the soap, and leave it for a while. Then scrub scrub scrub the stain when you wash the whole thing, properly by hand, or before you put it in the machine. On the package, from behind the name of the brand, a starburst so bright suggests you might be looking into the sun.

This is clean, the original, to-be-trusted, pure clean of clean.

*

There is a star-shaped hole in a backwards "R" in a non-grammatical sentence that has been merged into a terrible approximation of a single word, each jarring letter a different shade of colouring crayon.

It lets you buy some time away from your kids.
Until they want a new toy.

*

The room will have a bed. The bedding should be clean though will certainly be rougher than you like. The bathroom might be hygienic enough, but you can't be upset if it is not. There will be noise coming from somewhere all through the night. There might be a bread roll in a plastic packet and a slice of processed cheese for breakfast.

It's somewhere to sleep and you can't afford better.

*

We take the maize meal, and we cook it. Each family has its own way, and it also depends on the meal. Sometimes we like it loose and steaming, other times stiff so we can slice it into nice chunks, other times it must be crumbly so that you can press it into perfect mouthfuls with your fingers and dip it in relish. Behind the name on this packet, we can see a very happy big red star moving its limbs outwards, and then from the top right, there is an orderly line of little red stars tumbling down towards the big one. The last star in this little family is white and it sits inside the big red star, hovering perfectly just there above the "i" of the word, "white".

It is fortified with Vitamin A.
It is the country's favourite brand of pap.

*

A tidy man wears a neat jacket. He has an official-looking hat and a calm face. He is in the store buying bread. On his spotless lapel is pinned a modest dark green strip of felt, and a polished metal star.

It indicates that this soul has been saved.

*

A tourist is lost and needs directions. Seeing the star, she is relieved. She goes up to the young man. "Excuse me, Sheriff, which way to the Gautrain station?"

12

Forethought of Grief

Sarah Uheida

Don't resent sunset or sob skywards/ all is light and shadow/
nothing sacrificial/ about the moon that nightly loots light it cannot
keep/ and you: rare as star and more dependable/
forgive this perfect day/ its skies blued/ bruising Earth's clavicle/
first there was dust and dirt and now: field/ the warm green pulse
on the wrist of everything/ grassland and gasp love/ I flowerpress
mist to hide in your mouth, love/ dying
to save something for later/
language does not care for the ceremonies by which we know we've
lived/ often I borrow time I won't replace from the mouth of our only
sun/ what's one more gin/ when outside the day ends in excess/ and
inside the walls are pristine windows between you and the rising
night/ sunlight exits its own shimmering simmering reds and we're
in love/ all this animal happiness leaves us absentminded/
living each hour till living hurts/
mistaking mirrors for luminosities I can kneel and drink from/
extinction soaks my sleeve/ I do not have time for air/
in the kitchen peeling pomegranate hoping hunger can teach me
something/ forgetting straightaway/
if: minute by minute the nights are getting longer/
then: spring's nearing and it's aglow with amnesia/
giving way in your eyes are days days days/ pour them like paint

over poems you have no use for/ or bury them like fresh prey under the weight of tomorrow's hunt/
it's nightfall and night falls and no dusk is untouchable/
this world is all fabric and flesh and we feel it tearing/
some crevice of soft luminous unease that you try to hide from me/ the cat will crawl under the couch and the washing machine will break again and we will not have tried the WiFi feature you paid so much money for/ say something/ before the soot and before I lose you/ speak of the line from Peace of Wild Things/ and the serious stain of pomegranate juice so red and sure of its place in this life/ tell me of that time/
I *spoiled* the crème brûlée by sinking my spoon into softness/ skipping to the light that's inside everything/
you were furious and so in love/ whisper-yelled: *cracking the crisp caramel crust is what the whole damn dessert is about*/ I laughed sugar then/ could not untaste it into vanilla and salt or send it back to the kitchen/ to be able to say *I did not know* and mean *I smell sweet burning*/ learning the world is still ours to fail/ fail it with me come see me tomorrow/ all nocturnal and nectarous/ dismiss the dusk that will taste of caramel just before it smokes;

meet me inside that deepest shade of amber

let us be devoured there.

13

The Supernova Formula

Mzwakhe Xulu

The words echoed in Will's ears, becoming a relentless chant that refused to release its grip on his feeble mind.

"I am sorry, Dr Ackerman, but the university is letting you go ..."

Each repetition of those words was like a sledgehammer, crushing his spirit into the depths of despair. Grief, like a relentless storm, entwined with the alcohol that had just cost him his beloved job, became his only solace. The loss of his beloved wife, Taraji, a leading cardiologist at the University of Cape Town's Groote Schuur Hospital, had shattered his world. Memories of her fading away in the ICU haunted him—her life: a fragile thread, severed by the unforgiving consequences of a car crash.

A few months after Taraji's passing, he had sought solace in the counsel of a grief therapist. But each session had seemed to exacerbate his sorrow, leaving him feeling more desolate than before. It was as if grief therapy was an ill-fitting puzzle piece in the mosaic of his suffering. Will believed his grief needed a different kind of salve, and soon enough, alcohol had become his new confidant. Some days he had gone to work at the university intoxicated, a fact not lost on his colleagues and students. His friend, Professor Cynthia Mofokeng, who was also his supervisor as UCT's head of the astronomy department, had already warned him.

"Oh, come on Cynthia, it was just two glasses of whiskey. I don't know why everyone's on my case now. I just lost my wife, for goodness' sake!" he snapped when confronted.

"You're one of the finest astrophysicists I know, Will, and you're my friend. So, listen carefully when I say this: if the dean catches wind of this, I'll be caught between a rock and a hard place. Please, take some time off to process your grief and heal properly. This habit of showing up drunk here will cost you your job," she implored.

"Work is the only thing keeping me sane right now, Cynthia. I'll stop drinking before work, but I can't bear the thought of sitting at home doing nothing. Every time I close my eyes, I see T in the ICU ..." he began, only to trail off. "Staying home won't help," he confessed.

"Promise me you'll try, Will," she pleaded. "You should talk to your therapist about this. And you know you can talk to me, too. All you have to do is ask."

"I'll do my best, Cynthia," he promised. "Thank you for understanding."

Indeed, he stopped showing up at work intoxicated in the days after opening up to Cynthia. But then, one afternoon, a call from a travel agent triggered a descent back to the bottom of the bottle. Six months earlier, he and Taraji had been planning a vacation in Las Vegas, and the booking had been made, though not finalized. He had to cancel it now. After ending the call, he drove to the nearest liquor store and surrendered to the familiar embrace of alcohol. It wasn't long before he found himself ensnared by its clutches again, missing crucial work meetings and classes. When the university's patience wore thin, they severed the cord that bound him to his job. His lifeline. Not even Cynthia could save him this time without jeopardizing her position.

Days stretched into weeks, weeks into months, and Will sought refuge in his supernova work—a project he had started at UCT. He clung to the belief that he would one day return to lecturing, despite his tarnished record. When he wasn't writing, he drowned his sorrows in bottles of whiskey, the O' Jays, Teddy Pendergrass, and Barry White serving as the soundtrack to his melancholy. His devotion to alcohol only grew, despite it having cost him the one thing that still mattered after losing T. Inebriation became an unlikely muse, whispering words he couldn't utter sober. It offered solace without judgement, embracing him in moments where tears and vomit commingled. A testament to the depths of his sorrow.

During his tenure at UCT, Will lent his expertise as one of the lead astrophysicists to the South African National Space Agency (SANSA), delving into research on supernovas. He'd been leading a group of astrophysicists from five universities in South Africa, all working towards determining a model predicting the time of occurrence of supernovas and their advanced properties. There was still so much they didn't understand about them, and a few years earlier, because of his vast research experience into them overseas, he'd been asked by SANSA to lead the research project. His SANSA appointment had been linked to his tenure at UCT, and being terminated by the university meant he could no longer maintain his position at SANSA. However, even after his firing, his determination to contribute to coming up with a formula only grew. The formula would revolutionise his field and change the world.

Studying supernovas and predicting their occurrence would help them learn more about the universe as astrophysicists. Supernovas played a key role in the distribution of elements throughout the universe, elements that make up life. Will would often fly from Cape Town to SANSA's SALT (Southern African Large Telescope), based in the Northern Cape, to receive briefings from the operators tracking supernovas through the telescope. He would then coordinate with the team from the South African Astronomical Observatory for findings on supernova sightings.

Amid his writing and despair, he remembered one special morning he'd shared with Taraji in the sanctuary of their spacious dining room, when she had voiced her concern about his obsession with the work on supernovas.

"You'll drive yourself mad trying to solve this on your own, Will," she had gently admonished. "Isn't the research you do at SANSA enough? Why bring it home with you?"

"I'm on the verge of a breakthrough, T. So close!" Will had exclaimed, a grin adorning his face as he paced the room.

His unruly afro had swayed with his restless energy, and in that moment, he had envisioned a legacy—the Ackerman Supernova Formula. If successful, it would predict not just the timing but also the exact properties and distances of supernovas from Earth. It was important for them as astrophysicists to study and understand this sufficiently, as Will would often point out to his students how supernovas and other stars in the galaxy played an important role in the formation of new stars, planets, and all the other components of the universe. He could already see himself accepting a Nobel Prize in Physics for his groundbreaking work and being consequently named the father of modern astrophysics. Ambitious much?

Initially, Will had abandoned his formula. After Taraji's death, it had become a mere fantasy. Though he continued writing about supernovas, he removed any reference to the formula he once pursued. He was no longer interested in predicting their time of occurrence or similar properties. The hope the formula held had been extinguished alongside Taraji a month earlier.

One chilly Sunday morning, he woke up wet from the sweat that had been trickling throughout his body into his genitals. His heart thumped as though a hundred horses were galloping in it. Taraji had visited him in a dream. He had dreamt of her for the first time since her passing. He'd felt his stomach turning, sending him straight to the toilet a few times. Returning from the toilet, he felt different. Something new was growing inside of him. He didn't quite understand what he was feeling, so he couldn't explain it to you even if you'd asked. In the dream, Taraji had been furious with him, though he couldn't recall why. A dogmatic academic like him had never believed in communion with the dead through dreams, but her anger had shaken him. He'd never seen her that furious even when she was alive.

As he tried to decipher the dream's meaning, he was led to the Ackerman Supernova Formula he'd abandoned a while back. Rubbing his reddened eyes, he dashed to the home office and began entering variables into the Scilab computation program. His fingers flew across the laptop's keyboard. What he saw on the screen jolted his body with shock, freezing him in place. It couldn't be. Could it?

"This can't be. Let me substitute the gravitational constant variable with the geocentric gravitation constant one and see what happens!" Will's voice reverberated in his office, his calculations whirling like a maelstrom. Lightning-quick adjustments followed, and his laptop screen transformed into a canvas of frenzied typing. Hope and dread waged war on his face.

"No! No! No! It can't be. It just can't be! What if I swap the nominal solar constant with the nominal solar luminosity?" His face contorted with a mix of hope and dread. He returned to his desk, his hands typing feverishly, performing calculations with breakneck speed. His expression grew dour, lines etching deeper into his features. Then, he dialled a familiar number, waiting with bated breath for an answer.

"Hello, is that Michelle?" his voice quivered with urgency.

"Yes, this is she speaking." Michelle's voice sounded distant; a shadow of the warmth Will remembered. The coldness in her tone unsettled him, but he pressed on, determined to share his revelation.

"It's Will. Michelle, we need to talk," he implored, a sense of urgency woven into every word. Memories of their collaboration on the supernova research paper resurfaced their shared fascination with SN 1420.

"When I was fired from UCT, I was working on a formula predicting the time of supernova occurrences, as well as their distance from Earth's surface. Do you remember how we had to play around with the cosmological constant in the initial formula since it kept giving us a very large value, too large to apply to our calculations for Earth? Well, I think I've figured out how we should've done it. And if I'm right about this, then we have an existential crisis coming our way."

Silence hung heavy on the other end of the line, Michelle's voice betraying only a fraction of interest. "Ok ..." she responded, her tone guarded.

"I discovered something this morning that I can't share over the phone. It's sensitive. Can we meet at Alma?"

Will was asking to meet at the coffee spot they used to go for fuel and brainstorming during lulls in activity. Michelle understood the gravity of the request. Thirty minutes later, they found themselves in the familiar surroundings of The Alma Café in Rosebank, Cape Town. Will's eyes met Michelle's radiant gaze; the passage of time etched in their features. A mixture of surprise and concern coloured her voice as she greeted him.

"You look like you've seen a ghost," she remarked, curiosity mingling with apprehension.

Guiding her to a corner table, away from prying eyes, Will's hands trembled as he opened his grey HP laptop in a hurry. He kept glancing around him as if a certain someone was tailing him. Michelle wondered what was going on with her friend of more than a decade. She'd find out as soon as he stopped acting like a fugitive and settled down. They sat in silence for a moment, save the furious keystrokes. Moments later, they were both staring at the laptop screen. Will explained his discovery in hushed tones.

"Wait, if this is correct ..." Michelle's voice trailed off, her eyes gradually widening in disbelief. "A supernova will explode near our atmosphere in just ten days?"

"Yes. And it will be only thirty light years away," Will added. "Gamma rays from the supernova will most likely destroy the ozone layer. And since that protects us from ultraviolet radiation from the sun, it's likely to result in mutations in animals and people. Even atmospheric oxygen and nitrogen will be ionised, making the earth uninhabitable!"

"Oh my God we're looking at an apocalypse here!" Michelle exclaimed, her voice reaching a shrill pitch, earning them the stares of the couple seated at a nearby table.

"Lower your voice, Michelle. You still need to take this to SANSA to verify it."

"Of course," she replied. And here she began practising the deep breathing exercise for warding off a looming panic attack she had scoffed at during her last session with Dr Bhagwanth, her therapist.

Will knew his battle with alcoholism had tarnished his credibility. Nobody at SANSA would believe what he'd just discovered. So, he entrusted Michelle with the task of informing the agency about his discovery. They agreed not to disclose his findings to anyone else until Michelle had received verification and guidance from SANSA.

After parting ways with Michelle, Will incessantly checked his phone, awaiting one of the most important calls of his life. And three days later, it came.

"Hello?" Will answered, his heart pounding.

"Hello, Will, this is Lynn, assistant to the CEO of the South African National Space Agency," a squeaky voice responded from the other end of the line. "The CEO is sending a car to pick you up in an hour for a meeting with him and the President at Genadendal Residence."

True to their word, an hour later, an imposing black SUV arrived to take him to the president's residence in Cape Town. Upon his arrival, the President was in the middle of another meeting, so Will was directed to wait in the lobby. Soon, a bald middle-aged man and a young lady joined him in the lobby. After exchanging pleasantries, the lady made introductions.

"Will, we spoke on the phone. With me is Mr Katleho Dembe, SANSA CEO," she said, pointing to the bespectacled bald man. Will vaguely recognized him from his time at SANSA.

"Hello, Will," Katleho greeted, his voice carrying a tinge of sadness. "I wish I could say it's a pleasure to meet you, but given the circumstances, it feels inappropriate. We are about to meet with the President, the ministers of foreign affairs, state security, science and technology, defence, and two leading astronomers from the South African Astronomical Observatory. The minister told me that the President would like to hear directly from you, as the person who made this critical discovery."

"Thank you, Sir. It's an honour," Will responded, rising from his seat to shake the CEO's hand. As they continued making small talk, a door swung open from the President's office, revealing a lanky figure that Will recognized as the President's spokesperson.

"Gentlemen, welcome to Genadendal Residence. The President is ready to see you. Please follow me," the lanky young man in the black suit and dark sunglasses said, leading them into the President's office. At that moment, Will understood that there was no turning back. He was now walking into the President's office, where they would talk about the fate of the world. He nodded solemnly, a mixture of anticipation and foreboding dancing in his gaze. The world teetered on the brink of catastrophe, his discovery the catalyst of an impending crisis.

"Madam President, meet Dr Will Ackerman. Dr Ackerman meet the President and some of her cabinet members. And you remember your former colleagues from SANSA, Dr Williams and Dr Louw?"

"Yes, I do. It's a pleasure to meet you, Madam President," Will responded, taking the president's small but secure grip into his own ungainly, dewy hand.

"Right. Dr Ackerman, tell us whether we can survive this impending apocalypse or not, will you?" the President urged, her brown face wearing anticipation and uncertainty.

"Well, Ma'am, it's a bit tricky ..."

14

Africatown

Shamin Chibba

I got hired guns on my tail—so close I can smell them. I look over my shoulder, but nobody's there. These sons-a-bitches move like ghosts.

Former cops, I heard, who dropped their badges and turned to contract killing for more money. They won't find me here in Africatown. The place was never welcoming to cops, let alone cops-turned-killers.

I have an inkling who sent them. His name is Feng Bin: the biggest bloody gangster in the Shanghai-Suzhou Autonomous Region. I know why he wants me dead. I'm sleeping with his wife, Jody.

The pixel-juice is wearing off. Static hits my ears and my vision is pixelated. The paranoia is starting to kick in again. I reach into my peat coat and pull out another electro-dot and place it under my tongue. I feel a spark in my head. My nerves stand at attention. The razor-sharp focus returns, the static stops, my vision clears up.

The night is loud and sweaty. The Sanfu heat has settled on the streets. Fireworks go off everywhere, the sky is peppered with floating green lanterns, thousands of people wearing animal skull masks parade down every avenue. The noise makes it hard to forget it's Africatown Founder's Day. Fifty-one years now.

The Town is slap-bang between Shanghai and Suzhou. My customers find it hard to get to me. The highways and rail lines run above and around the town. The only ways in are through backroads and the solitary train stop on the outskirts on Kariba Street. But my customers are hot for the pixel-juice, and they come in droves. Most tourists come here to gratify some perverse urge for poverty porn. But all they find is all the colour, patterns, loudness, patience and beauty we brought from Africa. It is a town that can't sleep. It is the insomniac of China.

I run pixel-juice on these streets and business is banging. I can't go an hour without someone calling out, "Hey, Breezy," for a hit. Some say I'm a breath of fresh air. Others think I'm as foul as flatulence. Someone told me I got that nickname because I've earned their love.

I was born and raised in Africatown to South African immigrants. Both were killed during The Shopkeepers' Rebellion twelve years ago, when I was eighteen. I've lived alone in the family home ever since. It's a matchbox apartment on Nanyuki Alley.

The X-Com AR contact lenses start blinking. It's Jody. I take her call. Her face fills my bedroom.

"You got the tickets?" she asks.

"Yep. Booked through the X-Com. Two pax to Shanghai Pudong International on the maglev at eleven tonight then two flight tickets to Tashkent at three in the morning. And don't worry, you'll be safe. I made sure we can't be tracked. Meet me at Kariba Street Train Station at ten."

Earlier, I re-routed the X-Com via a proxy server I built. The signal pings in Buenos Aires, Interlaken, Paramaribo and a hundred other locations before it picks up both of our X-Coms. No one will know where we are or where we're going.

"I'm at the pub right now," she says. "Should be out in five minutes. I'll catch a hover-rickshaw. Feng Bin is in Suzhou for a business meeting. By the time he reaches the pub, we'll be long gone."

"The ghosts are closing in on me, I can feel it."

"One more thing: don't forget the money. A hundred-K will do."

"To start our life from scratch, I know. You've said a hundred times now."

"I sent you my account details a couple of minutes ago. Deposit it in there. If I get to the train station before you, I'll be waiting by the Africatown map. Look out for my purple coat."

"Yes, ma'am."

She hangs up. The bedroom reappears. I need to keep moving. If I stay any longer in this apartment, the ghosts will get to me. The Kariba Street station is a seventy-minute walk from my apartment. I dig into the fridge for the leftover Ghanaian-style jollof rice and plantain from last night. I scoff it down while standing, toss the paper bowl in the bin. Ghanian is better than Nigerian jollof any day. I switch the contact lenses to rest mode. I slip an isabile into my holster. It's a machete-like blade my father brought from South Africa. He snuck it into China—carried it to protect my mother and himself. When I took up Jow Ga Kung Fu as a teenager, I practised with the isabile and perfected it. I throw a peat coat over me. Wearing a coat on a hot night looks suspicious, I know, but I must hide the blade. I pat the pockets to make sure I have my product and leave the apartment, my family home. There's no time for goodbyes. I step onto Nanyuki Alley and into the Sanfu air. It taints my skin, but the drug keeps me cool, keeps me from sweating. The building stands between two food stalls—one selling Lagosian chilli goat stew and the other, South African umngqusho—samp and beans.

Ehiremen spots me and calls out "Ahoy" to get my attention. He's the one who runs the goat stew stall. He lifts his wildebeest mask and reveals a round face, with a smile interrupted by a chipped tooth. The elastic bands around his waist stretch to their max, having lost their tautness a long time ago. In school, the kids used to call him Quasimodo.

"Breezy, my fresh-aired bruv, how you dey? Got any of that juice for me?"

I find it hard to hear over the Afrobeats from his stall.

"You still owe me," I yell over the music.

"I'm a bit broke, man. See those people in the line for chop? It's going to be a good night. I'll have the money to you tomorrow morning."

"I can't advance you like this anymore."

"Abeg one more time, Breezy. You know I'm good for it."

"Okay, look, I'll square you up this way: if anyone who looks like a cop asks for me, get them off my tail."

"What double wahala you're in this time?"

"I can't get into it right now, situation is k-leg, man. You won't see me for a couple of days."

I drop a hit of pixel-juice in his hand and walk off. I must remain hidden, even in public. My X-Com picks up the bank accounts of hundreds of people walking the streets. I home in on a smug man who looks like money. He's got eleven-million yuan in his account. I help myself to just a hundred thousand—not enough for him to notice. I transfer almost all of it into Jody's account, keeping just enough to buy myself a few odds and ends where needed.

I find a stall selling one of these animal skulls. An old lady serves me. She walks in tune to Sona Jorbateh's kora she got going on the sound system. I choose the gemsbok mask. I like the way its horns point straight up with purpose.

"You plan on getting out of Africatown?" asks the old lady.

"How you ken, ma?"

"It's the way you walked in here—fast, fast, shoulders up to your ears."

"In another lifetime, you'd be my mother."

"And like your mother I'd say be careful wearing that mask outside our town. They want the cameras to see your face."

I drop twenty yuan on the counter. "Xiè xie," I say, and step off. I slip on the mask. I hear myself breathing and catch a whiff of the jollof rice I had earlier. I begin walking eastward to the train station.

Look, when I hooked up with Jody, I knew she was married. That was her disclaimer before we booked a hotel room on the shores of Lake Tai. I just didn't know her husband was Feng Bin. The man makes his money trading in wildlife, liquor and tobacco. But his biggest business is in pixel-juice. He gets it made and distributes it worldwide. It lands up in the hands of people like me—peddlers at the bottom of the drug's value chain.

I first met Jody at We Will Rock You, a pub she owns in Africatown's Okavango Avenue. It was a ballsy move on her part. Chinese-owned businesses didn't last here. I was peddling pixel-juice to the patrons outside, right beside the Chinese hookers who would call out to foreign men: "Hey handsome man, you want to buy me a drink?"

At first, Jody and I fought. A lot. she called me a colour wolf—a Chinese insult which loosely translated to pervert—and told me to get away from her bar. I reminded her that the pavement was public space. She threatened to call the cops, but never did. Now I know why. It was all a ruse. Had I not been peddling her husband's product; her bar wouldn't last longer than a month.

One day, she invited me inside, got me a drink, a watered-down Tsing Tao. She asked me to peddle the product inside the bar—that way, she still had feet through the door. It was a solid move because she then began making more money than ever before. Not long after she took a liking to me. We were left alone after closing one night and began to talk. She told me she gave up a career as a structural engineer to pursue the dream of having her own English-style pub. I told her the pub was the furthest I had been from home. She laughed.

The thing about Jody is her scent—you always knew she was nearby when you got a whiff of cinnamon and honey. I asked her to stay beside me all night because her perfume masked the more overwhelming smell of sweat left behind by the patrons. She thought I was funny. But I wasn't joking.

Our after-hours talks became a regular thing. She opened up about her husband going about as if she didn't exist, concerned only with his money. She wanted kids, he didn't. He was screwing around with expensive hookers shipped in from Vietnam. Men with money always screwed around, she said.

She liked the way I listened to her, without judgement, without the need to advise. She found that attractive. Then, one night, she leaned in, and I took the bait.

Cue bullshit lovemaking montage. At first, we'd fuck in the backseat of her car at the train graveyard that separated Africatown from Suzhou. Then things graduated to her office in the pub's loft. Eventually, we moved our nightly thrills to one of her apartments overlooking Lake Tai—about a ninety-minute drive from Africatown.

"He never comes to this apartment," she said. "It's where I come to unwind."

The conversation was blasé lovers talk: how much we loved each other, fantasising about running away together, starting over again. But one night, while we were chilling, she drinking a Shandong Cabernet Gernischt and I sucking on a Tsing Tao, out of nowhere, she blurts out something I didn't ken.

"You're noise, you know that?"

"You mean a nuisance."

"No, I mean, you are noise, like a bug, a glitch, an anomaly."

"What are you on about?"

"Nothing. Just thinking out loud. Don't hurt your brain, colour wolf."

Feng Bin never worried where she was. Only once did he call her while we were together. We were woken by the ringtone—some Mandopop girl band whined in my ear. He screamed at her. My Chinese is limited but it was something along the lines of "Where the fuck are you? It's eight in the morning. You're not at the pub." She said she needed to get away from the pub for a couple of days, left the keys with the manager and came to Lake Tai. I think he believed her because he calmed down and said he needed the keys to her office.

We joked around about running away together every now and then. But one evening, the joke turned into a serious idea. We started planning—looking for a perfect location, the right train time, the right date, the amount of money we would need, and even making provisions for hiccups in case there were any along the way. And that is how we found ourselves here, running to Tashkent in Uzbekistan. She wanted it to be an obscure place, where Feng Bin wouldn't even think of looking for her. The first locations she'd had in mind—Singapore, Hong Kong, Manila, Phnom Phen—were too risky. He had tentacles running throughout most of East Asia.

Last week, I noticed two Chinese guys parked in a hover-car across the road. They were watching me, and they wanted me to know it. Around the same time, I got a call from an unknown number. I thought it was a client. Turned out, it was Feng Bin. He spoke in a low calm growl.

"I know you're fucking my wife, Mr Breezy. That's a dangerous thing to do. You see those two men outside your building? I sent them. Former cops turned contract killers. They do as I say. They know you work for me. That's why you're not dead yet."

"I don't work for anyone. I run my own gig."

"That pixel-juice you run on the streets—all mine, Mr Breezy. I just get desperate fools like you to peddle it. I'll tell you what's going to happen: I'm going to dispense of you by the end of the week. And another desperate punk will replace you. I won't lose a dime."

He hung up. I was fucked. For the rest of the week, I didn't see the two killers or their car. But I could sense them. They were close. I'd go down to Ehiremen's stall, and I could see their shadows but not their forms. I'd go to sleep at night and hear their footsteps in my bedroom as if they were searching for something. I'd turn on the light and, sure as shit, the place would be empty. Like I say, they moved like ghosts.

A call comes through the X-Com. It's Ehiremen. His round face fills the street.

"Bruv, two Chinese guys pitched up here asking for you. They looked like cops—dirty types. I told them you were in Shanghai for the weekend. And why do you sound out of breath?"

"Which way did they go?"

"Up the street."

"Geez, did they go east, west, north, south?"

"No vex, bruv."

"Which way?"

"I don't know. Which way is Okavango?"

"Shit, it's west. They didn't believe you. They're heading to We Will Rock You."

"What're you on about?"

"You did good, man."

"We're square?"

"For sure."

His face disappears. I rip off my mask, turn and sprint westward in the direction of the pub. Thoughts flood my mind. They were after her all this time, not me. That phone call was meant to scare me away from her. But maybe she had left the bar already. They'd miss her. Or maybe they would bump into her. But Jody would be on a hover-rickshaw by then. She should be safe. But I can't take the chance. I must get to her before they do. And then it strikes me: what if they planned on trapping me at the pub? I stop running, process the thought. If they're after me, the best way to get to me is through Jody. I'm fucked.

Then I smell them, the ghosts. My peripheral vision picks up movement. I look over my shoulder. I'm the only one in the alley. Then a glass crushes underfoot. Cue bullshit chase scene. I bolt. My legs burn, my lungs burst. I go on. The footsteps behind me edge closer. I want to turn and look, but I can't. I hear a blast like a gunshot. Or could it be a backfiring vintage car? I can't tell. I must keep running. The pixel-juice is working overtime. I turn on the X-Com, yell into it to show me the quickest route to the Founder's Day parade. Blue arrows blink on the road in front of me. I amp up the pace. Their shadows run on the walls of the buildings, looming large and then disappearing. I turn left on Nakuru Road, right on Choba Street and right again on Tana Drive where the hordes are in their masks. I slow down, slip on the gemsbok mask and join the crowd. I lose the ghosts.

I'm part of the parade for three blocks before breaking away from it. I wave down a hover-rickshaw. "Take me to We Will Rock You pub on Okavango Avenue," I say. The driver says he knows exactly where it is. He tells me the cost. It's more than I expect. "It runs on uranium," he says. "That's why." I take it. The rickshaw moves, silent and clean. The pixel-juice dims in my system. The static hits. It drowns out the traffic. My vision becomes pixelated.

The driver reaches the pub before I take another hit of pixel-juice. The damage is thirty yuan. I tap my card. Insufficient funds. Fuck. I tell him I'll pay what I have on the card and cover the remainder with a hit of pixel-juice. He agrees. We make the exchange. I hop off the taxi and dart through the pub's door.

It's quiet inside—just the barman and some smoker at the bar watching rugby on mute. I walk up to the barman, who has on the skull of an impala as a mask. I ask for Jody. He seems nervous. "She's upstairs," he says. "Call her down," I say. He gets onto an old landline phone and speaks into it. "She's on her way," he says. "Xiè xie," I say.

I take a seat at a table and wait for her. My eye catches the guy at the bar wearing a white suit. His guise, the skull of a black-backed jackal, covers just his eyes and nose. He's got hair styled like a duck's ass and a pointy nose that is unusual for a Chinese guy. He doesn't look interested in the rugby. I try to fit in and hide the tension in my bones.

"Barman. Change the channel to the football, unless the gentleman at the bar is enjoying the rugby."

The smoker stubs out his cigarette.

"Where I come from 'gentleman' is a fighting word."

"Where's that?"

"Qingdao."

"Nice. I heard the beaches are great there and so is the fishing. Can I get you a drink?"

"I don't drink."

I laugh. "In China, everyone drinks."

"I don't drink," he says in a tone that puts an end to the menial chatter. He lights another cigarette and balances it between his lips as he speaks.

"Jody's not coming," he says.

"What'd you say?"

The guy turns to the barman and nods. He hands the barman a gun who then picks it up, points it to his chin and pulls the trigger. The bang fills the room. The barman's head whips back, his brain splatters against the wall, his body drops to the floor. Smoke rises through a hole in his impala mask.

My stomach churns. I was lured here. Fuck, I'm in double wahala. The static and pixelation surge. I crane my neck, stick my finger in my ear and rub hard. It doesn't help.

Then, as if the barman's ghost takes over his flesh, he stands up and looks at me through his mask. He steps away from the bar and disappears upstairs. I jump from my chair and step back.

"Don't worry about him," says Feng Bin as he pulls off his jackal skull and places it on the bar counter. "He'll serve you your Tsing Tao tomorrow with his head intact."

"He just fucking offed himself, man."

"I must thank your friend for sending you here. I guess money still buys loyalty in Africatown."

Fucking Ehiremen—Quasimodo twat bastard. I'm going to kill him when I see him.

"This world is not what you think it is, Mr Breezy."

I get to my feet and dash towards him. My hand reaches for the isabile under my coat. The two ghosts walk through the door on cue, guns in their hands. Feng Bin raises a hand. The ghosts relax. I pull my hand out of my coat.

"No need to spill blood just yet, gentlemen. Let's talk first, Mr Breezy."

"Get me Jody, now."

Feng Bin kicks up a stool and gestures me to sit. I choose to remain standing.

"She isn't here."

"Where is she?"

"Don't worry. She and the kid are where they're meant to be."

"Kid?"

A sudden iciness takes over me. The floor is yanked from under my feet and my world teeter-totters for a moment. I regain my composure. Feng Bin smirks.

"Goodness, you didn't know Jody was pregnant?"

"You're fucking with me."

"It doesn't perturb me that the two of you were sleeping together."

I regain my composure.

"So, if you don't care, let her go and we'll leave. We can forget this ever happened."

"I've told you before, screwing my wife was dangerous. The kid she's carrying, that's what frightens me."

I'm confused and he can see it all over my face.

"I knew you wouldn't be ready for the truth. But I have no choice but to tell it to you. Jody, you and I are NPCs."

"You're riddling me, man."

"We're non-playable characters."

"Like in videogames?"

"We are not living in a videogame. In 2038, China's ministry of state security employed a team of futurists and scenario planners to create an artificially intelligent digital simulation. I was the lead on that team. What you see before you, this bar, these men, and me: it's all an idea. As the team lead, I wrote myself into the simulation as a businessman. In this world, my methods might be a little unorthodox, but I'm still a businessman."

"You're a criminal."

"Businessman, criminal, it's hard to tell apart sometimes. Look at yourself, you tread that line with perfect balance."

The fucker had a point.

"Mr Breezy, here is the truth about this world: with the influx of African migrants coming into the country, the government wanted to find out what the repercussions would be if it left its borders open to such people. So, we designed a scenario: if African migrants fled to China, as they did, what would happen to its cities by the end of the century? The duration it assessed would be between 2040, when the simulation's development was complete, and 2100. We created a procedurally generated environment—an algorithm that would enable this world to grow automatically, the same way towns would organically grow into cities in the real world. And we found that African migrants would concentrate in a remote area where they could feed off the economy of an established major city. We placed the migrants within a four-block radius between Shanghai and Suzhou. What we found was that, because of China's growing

115

economy, more Africans would flock to China for new opportunities. Eventually, we found that the town would grow by fifty per cent within eight years, and a hundred per cent within fifteen years. By 2089, the year you are in now, it is a fully fledged city. There would be an African diaspora born and raised here, knowing nothing of their mother continent, or of their ancestors, much like you. We expected violence, debauchery, and all kinds of perversions—you know, all of the stereotypes we'd heard about Africa. Instead, we found a well-organised, cooperative and colourful community. The only thing we found difficult to control was the people's volition and their penchant for political, economic and civic freedom. Which is why the government has decided to maintain its conservative migration policy in the real world. All resident Africans are now to be deported.

"But amidst all of this, there was an anomaly. Something we did not expect. That static and pixelation you are experiencing right now—that is what you are, light and sound. Pure information. Except, of all the NPCs in this world, you are that anomaly."

Jody had said the same thing. I let him speak.

"In communication theory, for an encoded message to be successfully decoded at its destination, it needs to travel across the system unimpeded. Seldomly, an anomaly occurs, that of noise, which changes an encoded message. So, when it reaches its destination—be it a listener, reader or viewer—it is sure to be decoded incorrectly. The noise can be a distortion in a visual feed, static in radio transmission, or even a sneeze from an orator. About three years ago, this country's massive FAST radio telescope, in the Dawodang Basin, picked up a massive coronal mass ejection from the sun, accompanied by a solar flare. Nothing unusual, they said. It happens all the time, they said. Except, this one was so strong, it affected most communication devices on Earth, including the system of servers in which Africatown resides. The scientists said the burst lasted half-an-hour. It was the only information they offered to the public. But they deliberately left out a peculiar detail because they didn't want the public and the market to panic when they found out. They figured that digital communication systems all over the world had suddenly been infected with bugs. Some had minor effects, but other incursions were so devastating, servers would be shut down for good. Digital environments were warped to an unrecognisable degree. Worlds killed off in an instant. In our digital environment, that of Africatown, an NPC was added, one that should not have been here. And that is you, Mr Breezy. You are the noise."

I'm trying hard to keep up with what he is saying. My chest tightens and my breathing shallows.

"I don't expect you to understand everything I've just said. All you really need to know is that you don't belong in Africatown."

"Bullshit. I was born and raised on Nanyuki Alley. I watched this town grow from four blocks with a few thousand expats to a town of hundreds of thousands."

"This world is not made of gas and dust as we are meant to believe. The town and the NPCs are binary numbers, ones and zeroes, and Africatown expands automatically because my team incorporated machine learning into this environment. You believe your thoughts are yours, but the fact is we created the code that would enable all of you to think like real human beings—with its mixture of logic and chaos. And the more information we added to the environment, the more human-like the NPCs became. They started having their own thoughts, desires and ideas. For instance, you and Jody had the brilliant idea of running away to Tashkent. It was unexpected but I got so much joy from watching the two of you plan it out. I felt that, finally, a creation of mine was turning into an independent organism. Unfortunately, for you two, the tickets to Tashkent— they're not real. There is no Tashkent in this world. The rest of China doesn't exist here. There is nothing beyond the Shanghai-Suzhou Autonomous Region. Shanghai Pudong International is outside the region's limits. So, if you were to leave on the maglev train as you had planned, the moment you got out of the limits, you would fall through an abyss and land right back in Africatown. There is no reality other than this, Mr Breezy."

I wonder if I'm not overdosing on pixel-juice right now and imagining all the shit he's saying. It can't be, though. I'm as hyper-focused and clear-minded as I've ever been.

"We detected you early on in the experiment and I thought you were too minor a bug to be of much concern, yet you seamlessly assimilated into the simulation. When you started sleeping with Jody, I left the two of you alone. I was curious about the result. But allowing you to remain in the simulation was a mistake on my part. I didn't foresee that a minor bug latching onto Jody, a regular NPC, would create a virus—your progeny—that could destroy Africatown. Your child has the ability to override the server, break the simulation and cost the state billions. The experiment would be a failure. I could not let that happen."

"I'm not a bug and my kid isn't a virus."

"It doesn't matter what you believe, Mr Breezy. What matters is the extermination of the virus in this world. These are the anti-viruses."

He pointed to the two ghosts.

"I can confirm they've cleared Africatown of the virus. Now, they just need to erase the bug."

The ghosts reach for their guns. My body wants to run, but my brain calms it down. My breathing slows, the hairs all over my body stand erect. All my Jow Ga training has prepared me for this singular moment. I whip out the isabile from under my peat coat and at the speed of sound, I bring the blade across my body, backhanded, and slit Feng Bin's throat. Blood splatters across my face and soaks his white suit. The ghosts take aim. I jump over the bar counter to take cover. I'm a little slow. A bullet strikes my left shoulder. It burns like a branding iron. I remain behind cover until they run out of bullets. It is my only chance to run. I skip over the counter and with one sweep of the blade cut open their chests. I shoulder charge them, rugby-style, and drop them on the blood-soaked floor. I burst out of the pub and into traffic. Cars and bikes dodge me. I manage to stop a hover-rickshaw. I quickly hop on. I tell him to take me to Kariba Street Train Station fast. The ghosts are back on their feet and at the door. The gunshots scare the rickshaw driver into pressing his foot to the floor and zooming down Okavango. The driver cusses at me, tells me the vehicle got hit and the ride will cost me my entire life's savings. I tell him I have no money, that I'll pay him in pixel-juice. He asks me three times if I'm lying to him. I show him the package. He drives like a demon and within minutes, we're outside the station. I hand him two electro-dots. He slips them under his tongue straight away and scoots.

I slip on the gemsbok mask and enter the building. I follow the signs to the maglev train. It's four levels down. I take the stairs. The train pulls up like an oversized iron earthworm on speed, blowing back my hair and my peat coat.

I hop on and take a seat at the front of the car. I breathe. The train starts to move, slowly at first, then it picks up speed. The digital speedometer on the wall says it is moving at four-hundred kilometres per hour and tops out at five-fifty-four. We're about to reach the outer limits of the autonomous region when there is a tap on my shoulder. Two conductors in blue stand over me, looking official and lacking volition. One of them tells me to take off the mask.

"I can't," I say. "I'm playing hide-and-seek with a friend."

The other guy asks me why I'm wearing a coat on such a hot night.

"Don't you know, this is a sailor's coat? I'm going sailing as soon as I hop off the train."

One of them rolls their eyes and says, "Come with us." I refuse. They threaten to kick me off at the next stop if I don't take off the mask. I laugh and tell them to go fuck themselves. One of them grabs me by the arm. I elbow him in the face, the other returns the favour with bare knuckles. They lift me up and carry me between them. I kick, I scream, I laugh. "It's a joke," I yell.

And then the train falls, down a hole, into an abyss. And all goes black. I feel weightless as I fall through the air. My arms flail, panic sets in. In a desperate attempt to seek comfort, I tell myself it's all a joke. It doesn't work. The static dies, the pixels disappear, I become light and sound. From above I see a seven-headed snake coil itself around Africatown. People dance in circles and chant a dirge. Then a lotus flower. A million petals open. Inside is a ten-headed man, sitting and meditating. I see into his mind. He is creating and destroying worlds a thousand times over. I enter the mouth of a galaxy, jets streaming through its centre. I enter another mouth, and then another and another, until I wake up. I rub my eyes. I'm back in my bedroom. I jump out of bed and step over the gemsbok mask on the floor. I saunter to the window and see Nanyuki Alley below, busy as usual. And across the street stands Feng Bin with the ghosts behind him. The fucker looks up at me. He smiles and nods.

15

As Above, So Below:
Outroductory Reflections on FicSci 02

Wamuwi Mbao and Mehita Iqani

FicSci playfully subverts the words 'science' and 'fiction' which are most often glued together in the term 'science-fiction', that genre of narrative fusing literary and popular appeal that tests and explores the limits of imagination in relation to scientific possibility (and vice versa). The huge realm of science-fiction (sf) literary scholarship asserts that it is less a genre than an ongoing *discussion* (James and Mendlesohn 2003, 1). Rooted in a similar interest in the relation between fiction and science, FicSci initiates its own ongoing discussion that starts with a recognition of the value that creative and experimental writing can bring to the scientific project, rather than the perhaps often assumed other way around (that is, that science inspires fiction). This anthology offers the second iteration of the ongoing discussion that is FicSci, and in these comments we offer a few "outroductory" comments (rather than introductory, as we have forged these through a process of looking back on the works that were written during the workshop) on what this discussion means in the context of both creative writing and science communication.

The question of what science can learn from creative writers is not new. Many scientists have crossed over into that realm of enquiry from backgrounds in writing training, or paused to muse on what good writing skills might offer their own projects of connecting their findings with publics (Gross 2017), including, specifically, astronomy (Fraknoi 2003). Science communication experts have also written about the possibilities attendant to introducing writerly tricks of the trade into the dissemination of scientific research (Joubert et al. 2019).

FicSci is an experiment in hybridized creative practice that induces new forms of knowledge-making between the hard sciences and the social world. The FicSci project is about finding ways to amplify the resonance of scientific happenings into ordinary life via the interpretive work of a cohort of diverse creatives. In the first part of the project, the cohort attends an immersive workshop with a scientist who shares their knowledge in several ways. Over the course of three days, we follow ideas around together, and think collectively at the seam where scientific concepts meet the fabric of living. We are invited to dwell within the reverb of scientific ideas: that dwelling might involve questioning, speculating, discovering points of connection, practising absorption and engagement, and other modes of knowledge proximity. Sitting with a scientist and engaging them on their ideas produces new curiosities about the way science appears in the world. When we think with science in this way, we activate the possibility of making dynamic connections with our own knowledges and histories.

A very famous scientist turned public intellectual and, like our FicSci 02 provocateur, also an astronomer active on social media once commented on Twitter that "the universe is under no obligation to make sense to you" (@neiltyson, 3 April 2021). This is not untrue. But perhaps Neil DeGrasse Tyson had yet to appreciate how all forms of writing, including the humble tweet, indeed all forms of human creative expression, from carving out shapes on trees to sophisticated musical composition, are exercises in trying to make sense of the complexities of in-universe experience, of which the human is only a (small) part.

The quest to make sense—in any of the modalities available to human cognition and sensory tools, including the emotional—is arguably one of the key driving forces of narrative practice. Creative writers working in any genre seek to unlock aspects of the human condition to make sense of experience, not in the form of logically unpicking linear forms of cause and effect, but in terms of exploring and inhabiting complex forms of entangled meaning. While the FicSci cohort is gathered, we compose an improvisational creative encounter that explores, translates, and stories science in our own formats, be that poetry, prose, visual art, or other dynamic and expressive craft forms. The project becomes a kind of conceptual laboratory in which the act of listening to a scientist speak and think about the technical dimensions of their work creates a generative environment in which we might each find our own relation to what we hear.

For some of the participants, science is something distant and incoherent that belongs to its own world, an insular world whose logics and rhythms are understood and inhabited only by people whose expressive energies are not in sync with our own. Science is, we imagine, a serious discipline: enigmatic yet heavily factual, resistant to banality and fantasy. Our relationship to it is primarily only at the level of the descriptive, which seems inadequate and uncomfortable. But to stay in proximity with what we don't know, and more importantly, to take seriously our own relation to science even as it seems arcane, is to navigate our relationship to science in ways that are vitalizing and necessary. This is to say that the workshop is also a kind of methodological experiment, where the methodologies for storying the scientific encounter are creatively multi-form. Someone might choose to draw their way through; someone else might choose to use poetry to describe how they were moved by science. The cohort embraces a spirit of generous collaboration: we are all (including the scientist) taking time out of our lives and schedules to listen, to discuss, to think through, and to create.

The cohort emerges from the three days with a more capacious sense of how science might be tied to the imagination. Our collaborative efforts during the workshop create a structure of atypical connections: we create work that is attendant to the wider potentialities of scientific thought. This anthology materializes that work.

How different, really, are the yearnings of astronomers and writers, in relation to the stars? DeGrasse Tyson, surely one of the most quoted celebrity scientists of all time, is also oft-cited in his explanations of how

> the very molecules that make up your body, the atoms that construct the molecules, are traceable to the crucibles that were once the centers of high mass stars that exploded their chemically rich guts into the galaxy, enriching pristine gas clouds with the chemistry of life (Edwards and Gaber 2014, p. 5).

In other words, as above, so below. Many things can be written in the stars; in fact, anything that is possible to be expressed by human cognition already is. And that might be precisely why human beings cannot resist producing both science and fiction regarding the night sky.

We petty humans, our loves and lives, our hearts and guts, our triumphs, our losses, are produced from the same substances that ignite the countless shimmering lights in the night sky. When we gaze up, we gaze into our own souls: this is not a metaphor. Every human capacity to learn, understand, communicate and create is produced by the material properties of our bodies and brains (Seth 2021). If our brains, including their capacity to produce the still little-understood complexities of our psychic, narrative, and emotional worlds, are made of the same stuff as stars, then it is no surprise that looking up at the night sky takes writers into deep personal terrain, as well as the more prosaic territories of sf that are already well-animated by the ongoing discussion of the genre.

The collection of writing that resulted from the FicSci 02 encounter with astrophysics explores multiple aspects of human relationality and agency and seems more tied to matters of this earthly plane than might be expected (dating, politics, addiction, family, childhood, contraception, branding, heartache).

What we see when we look up at the stars is ourselves reflected.

References

Edwards, Kieran Jay, and Mohammed Medhat Gaber. *Astronomy and Big Data: A Data Clustering Approach to Identifying Uncertain Galaxy Morphology*. Cham, Switzerland: Springer, 2014.

Fraknoi, Andrew. "Teaching Astronomy with Science Fiction: A Resource Guide." *Atronomy Education Review* 1, no. 2 (July 2002—January 2003): 112–19.

Gross, Kayla. "What Scientists Can Learn From Fiction Writers." *Tufts Boston Insight*, April 10, 2017. https://sites.tufts.edu/insight/2017/04/10/what-scientists-can-learn-from-fiction-writers/

James, Edward, and Mendlesohn, Farah, eds. *The Cambridge Companion to Science Fiction*. Cambridge; New York: Cambridge University Press, 2003.

Joubert, Marina, Davis, Lloyd and Metcalfe, Jenni. "Storytelling: The Soul of Science Communication." *Journal of Science Communication* 18, no. 5 (2019): E. https://jcom.sissa.it/article/pubid/JCOM_1805_2019_E/

Seth, Anil. *Being You: A New Science of Consciousness*. London: Faber & Faber, 2021.

Biographies

Alicia English is an award-winning entrepreneur and editor, and a Mitchell's Plain mother of three boys. She is the author of childrens' books *Shanté and the Whale* and *Mahalia the Rainbow Princess*. She runs her own publishing business The Olive Exchange and devotes her time to raising awareness about child grief, encouraging children to write their own stories, and improving reading comprehension among primary school learners in the Cape Flats. Alicia started her writing career as a young journalist in 1998 and has since worked as a newspaper journalist and magazine editor on several magazines.

Eduardo Cachucho is the Creative Director for the Fak'ugesi African Digital Innovation Festival. He is a programme consultant, artist and ex-architect. He has worked in digital innovation in the creative sector for over a decade both locally and internationally, believing that digital creative practices are the key to sustainable empowerment in South Africa and the African continent. As an artist he works in a few key mediums: performance, drawing, and speaking/writing. He has particular interest in language, subjectivity, and high level concepts in culture and science, particularly in creating models to make these concepts understandable to the public.

Maneo Refiloe Mohale is a South African editor, feminist writer and poet. Their work has appeared in various local and international

126

publications, including *Jalada, Prufrock, The Johannesburg Review of Books, The Mail & Guardian*, spectrum.za, and others. They were Bitch Media's first Global Feminism Writing Fellow in their inaugural 2016 class, where they wrote on race, media, sexuality and survivorship. They have been long-listed twice for the Sol Plaatje European Union Poetry Anthology Award, and their debut collection of poetry, *Everything is a Deathly Flower* was published by uHlanga in September 2019. The book was shortlisted for the Ingrid Jonker Poetry Prize, later winning the 2020 Glenna Luschei Prize for African Poetry.

Mathapelo Mofokeng is a writer from Johannesburg, South Africa. Her writing has appeared in *Gagosian Quarterly*, the *Kenyon Review Journal, Adda Magazine*, and *Popshot Quarterly*, among others, and has been anthologised in the Pen America Dau Prize's *Best Short Stories 2021* and the *Future of Media*. She is a recipient of the Pen/ Robert J. Dau Short Story Prize for Emerging Writers, as well as fellowships from Macdowell, the Camargo Foundation, the Miles Morland Foundation, and Chevening.

Melissa Sussens is a queer South African veterinarian and poet. Her debut collection, *Slaughterhouse*, was published by Karavan Press in 2022. She placed 2nd in the 2020 New Contrast National Poetry Prize and was shortlisted for the 2022 prize. She was selected as one of the winners in the ClemenGold Writing Competition in 2020 and was one of the shortlisted poets for the Time of the Writer: Poetry For Human Rights competition in 2021. Her work has appeared in many publications, both locally and internationally, including SFWP Quarterly, Kissing Dynamite, AVBOB Poetry and Isele Magazine, among others. Sussens has twice been nominated for Best of the Net and has performed at Off the Wall, Poetry in McGregor and The Commons. She will lead a poetry workshop at Open Book Festival and is part of The Red Wheelbarrow Poetry Collective where she helps to host poetry readings and open mics. When she is not doctoring small animals, Melissa is a teaching assistant for Megan Falley's online writing course, Poems That Don't Suck and does freelance poetry editing. She lives in Cape Town with her spouse and their two dogs. Find her at melissasussens.com or @melissasussens.

Mzwakhe Xulu is is a multi-talented individual with interests in entrepreneurship, innovation and writing. He leads LaTonisi Business Consultants, a business development services agency based in Durban, KwaZulu-Natal, while also managing operations at CulinearClear Solutions and spearheading Hydrowize Solutions Pty Ltd, a water management solutions start-up. Dedicated to youth development, in 2016 he co-founded Calibrating Minds Society NPO, focusing on debating and career expos for learners in Empangeni and Newcastle in KwaZulu-Natal. Additionally, Mzwakhe serves as deputy chairperson on the board of the KwaZulu-Natal Schools Debating Association. His remarkable contributions have earned him several awards, including the 100 South African Shining Stars Award, Mail & Guardian's 200 Young South Africans, Africa's 100 Brightest Young Minds, Sunday World's Unsung Heroes, Unleash Innovation Lab, and the UNISA Innovation Challenge.

Peggy Tunyiswa is a Fleur Du Cap Theatre Award winning actress. She left her home in Keiskammahoek to pursue her dreams to build a theatre there. She trained in Theatre and Performance at the University of Cape Town. Since graduation she has appeared in local and international productions of film, theatre, commercials, audiobooks, animation, and art installations. She values entrepreneurship, community development, arts and business, and activism. Her Industrial Theatre company runs awareness campaigns for financial wellness, drug and alcohol abuse, saving money for children and youth, and digital transformation for artists. She writes, directs, facilitates, and produces individually and in collaboration. She regularly shows collaborative work at performance art festivals. She is a champion for diversity, equality, equity and inclusion for minority groups and underserved communities. She is proud of her roots and has created a niche for herself working in her mother language isiXhosa as a reviewer, praise poet, dialogue and acting coach and a director in plays and audiobooks.

Sarah Uheida is a Libyan poet and experimental memoirist currently pursuing her Master's in English studies at Stellenbosch University. At the age of thirteen, Sarah and her family escaped the Libyan Civil War and migrated to South Africa, where she first learned English and is currently residing. As the recipient of the international 2020 Miles Morland scholarship, she is currently penning a fictionalised memoir of the Libyan Civil War and the female refugee experience. She was the recipient of the 2020 Dan Veach Prize for Younger Poets. Her work features in or is forthcoming in a selection of literary anthologies which include HarperCollin's HarperVia, New Contrast, Atlanta Review, Eunoia Review, The Shore, fresh.ink, Plume, the South African, Sonder Midwest, Stone Thursday, Every Day Fiction, Wend, Flock, and in the anthology We Call to the Eye and the Night: Love Poems by Writers of Arab Descent, which Persea Books published in 2023.

Shamin Chibba badly badly wanted to be a professional footballer, but sucked at it. Instead, he found a talent for telling stories through words and pictures. A professional member of PEN South Africa, he has been a feature writer for various publications, a graphic novelist, a playwright and a short story writer. He is also a visual artist.

Skye Ayla Mallac is a poet, journalist and creative writer whose major influences are the landscapes of Southern Africa. Having written a short fantasy novel in high school, she went on to study journalism and has worked extensively within the music, entertainment, sustainability, and regenerative spheres. In February 2022 she published her debut collection of poetry *Whole, Gold, Crystalline* which is stocked in bookshops across the country. Over the course of three months at the end of 2022 she wrote the first draft of a Southern African fantasy novel which she is currently editing with the intention to publish. Her core focus is on shedding light on ecosystemic collapse within the fynbos region through her creative writing.

Taryn Mackay (aka memory's daughter) is a PhD fellow. Her research is focused on mother-hood as a technology of practice that can provide pathways to deeply relational thinking as practised by Indigenous Knowledge Systems (IKS). Mackay's roots her research and practice in socio-political activism and positioning social justice as the framework for knowledge production.

Yolanda Mbelle was born in Boksburg, Benoni in Ekurhuleni, South Africa. She grew up in Daveyton before moving to spend most of her childhood in another Ekurhuleni township, Tembisa. Her fascination with people and the love she has for storytelling led Yolanda to seek to learn more about people by working with them through television and community work. She launched a magazine called The Ambassador and has worked on several television and film productions, including Ambassador TV, I Survived on SABC 2, Capture, Siembamba, Blood Psalms, and the Varsity TV Presenter Search. She was co-founder of Oncue Interface TV Presenter Training and later up to date founded the OMG (Obakeng Media Group) and went on to be recognized as an influential woman in the film and TV industry by the Gauteng Film Commission. She also offers training for film and television personalities.

Editors

Mehita Iqani is an academic researcher and writer in the field of media, communications and cultural studies, in which she has published widely. She is currently based in the Journalism Department at Stellenbosch University, where she runs research projects on climate and environment, health and happiness and creative communications through the DSI-NRF-funded SA Research Chair in Science Communication, of which she is Chairholder.

Wamuwi Mbao is a writer and literary critic. He teaches literature at Stellenbosch University. His research interests are in South African popular culture, literary criticism, mid-century modern architecture, and automotive histories. He is the editor of *Years of*

Fire and Ash: South African Poetry of Decolonization. He is a fiction critic with the Johannesburg Review of Books. His work has appeared in various publications. His short story "The Bath" was noted as one of the most significant short stories of South Africa's new democracy. He is the recipient of a South African Literary Award for his body of literary criticism.

Invited Scientist

Tana Joseph is a South African astronomer, entrepreneur, public speaker and social justice advocate for the sciences. She obtained her PhD in physics in 2013 and has been awarded both Fulbright and Royal Society fellowships in recognition of her research excellence. She is passionate about science communication and firmly believes that science is for everyone. In 2018, she founded her own science, technology, engineering and maths (STEM) communications and consulting company, AstroComms. She is an advocate and consultant for EDI and decolonisation efforts in astronomy and science. In this capacity, she works as the Equity and Inclusion coordinator for astronomy in the Netherlands.

www.ingramcontent.com/pod-product-compliance
Lightning Source LLC
Chambersburg PA
CBHW052012270326
41929CB00015B/2886